Why a Church catholic?

John D. Garvey, S.J.

Sheed & Ward

Sheed & Ward™ is a service of National Catholic Reporter Publishing Company, Inc.

Library of Congress Catalog Card Number: 87-61052

ISBN: 1-55612-063-X

Published by: Sheed & Ward
115 E. Armour Blvd., P.O. Box 414292
Kansas City, MO 64141-4292

To order, call: 800-333-7373

Contents

Preface

This book is written to prove a thesis, a thesis I have become more and more convinced of over a long academic career in the field of Christian theology and I want to set down the reasons for my conviction in the hope that they might help others as much as they have helped me in meeting the challenges which the modern intellectual world poses to Christian faith. The fact that it is unknown or overlooked by many of those who need it most, and even contradicts some popular assumptions, makes me more anxious to propose and defend it. In scholarly theological circles what I am saying substantially throughout this work is anything but new; in fact, it is almost commonplace. Still what is commonplace among theologians is not always known and appreciated by those who, while well educated in other fields and alert to the general trends in our culture, are unfamiliar with theological literature. This book is addressed to them.

Chapter One

What It Means to Be Catholic

Simply put my thesis is that it has never been more important than at present for Christians to be catholic. Just to state such a proposition will surely raise the hackles of many a reader, but I am convinced that it is true and thoroughly defensible. Of course, the proposition needs explanation and qualification and the first chapter attempts to provide such. For the moment, I am satisfied to set forth plainly the major contention which subsequent chapters will try to explain and establish.

One qualification needs to be made at once, however. The word "catholic" in the title is written with a small letter. It is not a proper noun, naming a particular church, but an adjective describing the church of Jesus Christ wherever it is found. Many Christians who are not Roman Catholics profess faith in the holy, *catholic* church, according to the ancient creeds, so the Catholic Church (with capital letters) does not hold exclusive title to the name. This book is not intended, therefore, as a polemi-

1

cal defense of the Roman Catholic Church as she exists today, though I am and intend to remain a loyal member of that church. My purpose here is wider than that. Moreover, much current practice within the Catholic Church (written with capital letters) can be criticized in the name of catholicity. So this book can be read as both an argument that all Christians need to be catholic and an invitation to my own Roman Catholic community to be more fully what her name demands. That the Roman Catholic Church has unique qualifications to be what her name implies and thus to render an important and especially timely service to all believers is the theme of the last section in Chapter One.

Let me clear the field of one further expectation which the topic of this book might suggest. It is not a history of catholicity as that notion has developed over the centuries nor a profound theological analysis of the notion itself. My starting point is the understanding of catholicity as it exists today after centuries of development. I shall explore this notion in more detail in the following chapter but leave to better scholars in Christian history the task of tracing its origins and the vicissitudes of interpretation it has undergone since the word first emerged in the works of Ignatius of Antioch about the beginning of the second century.[1]

In one sense the catholicity we are talking about is an ideal and an abstraction. Like holiness and other qualities that Christian faith attributes to the church, catholicity describes the church as she will be when Jesus' victory will be complete at the *parousia*; it has never been and will never be fully realized in history. As an ideal and an assignment the call to be catholic points out the direction we should go, it does not mirror the actualities of Christian life now. The essential motivation to press on in that direction is faith, not the tangible evidence of what Christians have done in the world around us. So we cannot turn to the historical record or present Christian practice for an unambiguous picture of the catholicity at issue.

But it is only in a limited sense that catholicity is an ideal and an abstraction. In a very basic way Christianity is always about history. It is not about some theoretical ideals or some mythic vision which could inspire our actions, but about God's presence in our real and concrete world, through the risen Christ and in the Spirit. The kingdom of God has begun amongst us and therefore the catholicity which ought to characterize it must be related to the actualities of the world as we know it from experience. We shall try to do this relating in the pages which follow.

First we shall explore the meaning of catholicity. If the description seems too abstract and theoretical, I ask the reader's indulgence, because the word "catholic" is deceptively simple. It seems necessary to untangle some of the stands woven into its meaning before we examine how it applies to the church. As our investigation proceeds we will get down to particulars.

A final preliminary observation is in order. Religious statistics seem to contradict the thesis advanced in this book. The movements among Christians which seem most flourishing today tend to be narrow and sectarian rather than catholic, and whereas catholicity necessarily emphasizes the social and communitarian side of religion, organized religion and the formal agencies and institutions of the churches appear to have fallen on hard times at least among some of the more influential segments of our society. Nonetheless I believe the thesis stands because it rests on grounds which are independent of popular trends. It derives from the challenge posed to Christian belief by the intellectual currents of the modern world—a challenge which cannot be evaded. It is my contention that this challenge can only be met satisfactorily by a religion which is catholic. The individual believer can have such unshakable conviction that no objection can penetrate his or her defenses. He can even cling tenaciously to positions which are totally unacceptable in the light of modern knowledge rather than compromise his faith, but erosion is inevitable, if not within the religious history of the individual at least when faith is transmitted to others. The tension between a faith and a secular culture totally out of alignment with each other is ultimately intolerable. This is not to say, of course, that Christian faith cannot and should not be counter-cultural, in the best sense, but that the relation between Christian faith and the prevailing views and values of contemporary humanity at large must be intelligent and articulate, even when in contradiction. In the long run believers cannot simply ignore the world of which they are a part. They must be able to "give a reason for the faith that is within them,"[2] and for this purely individual piety will not suffice. The support of the wider "catholic" community is essential. It is essential, too, for other needs even more urgent than assuring the reasonableness of faith, as we hope to show in the course of this work. In our day evidence is converging from all sides to show that fragmented individualism in religion as in other domains is unhealthy and irresponsible. Distances and barriers between people, internal as well as external, are shrinking. In religion as in international relations mankind is being summoned to a new level of community and cooperation as the price of survival. From its earliest beginnings the Christian religion has claimed to be catholic, but I believe it is peculiar to our own times to find in that catholicity the precise characteristic of the Christian religion which responds most directly to its own special needs.

From the early creeds in which they confessed their faith, believers proclaimed that the church of Jesus Christ is "catholic." What did they mean by this and what are its implications? According to the dictionary *catholic* means universal or "pertaining to the whole" as opposed to partial, factional or sectarian. A group will be more catholic the less restricted its membership and an individual will be more catholic the wider his or her interests and the more capable of assimilating what is new and different. Catholicity is the ability and eagerness to grow in every dimension. We speak about a person of catholic or cosmopolitan tastes, one who is interested in everything, receptive to beauty and value wherever they appear, unlike a narrow minded person, whose horizons are bounded by the limits of his own group or nation or class.

This is pertinent to the Christian understanding of the word but it does not do full justice to the quality which has been recognized as a mark or sign of the church of Jesus Christ, rooted not in statistics or temperament but in the very essence of the church as faith sees her. To Christians the church was catholic while all its members were still in Jerusalem. The church is catholic because she is the body of Christ and no one comes to the Father except through Christ. The catholicity of the church is a consequence of the Incarnation and you cannot deny one without denying the other. The church is catholic because there is only one plan of God for all mankind and that plan converges upon Jesus. He is the *alpha* and the *omega*, the one who brings to completeness all the scattered beginnings of God's work in the world at all times and in all places.

There is a profound analysis of catholicity in a significant and influential book by Henri de Lubac,[1] and the interested reader will find there much of the early Christian literature on the subject. Catholicity is openness. It is the capacity to receive from all peoples and all cultures and to transform what it receives. It is the quality of leaven that can permeate the dough of humanity and all that humanity touches. It is the power of expansion, but not imperialistic expansion, rather one which is itself molded while it molds. It is an influence that does not denature but enables all that it touches to become more truly itself. Congar expresses it well, when he says that the catholicity of the Church is "the dynamic universality of her unity: the capacity of her principles of unity for assimilating, fulfilling, exalting, winning for God, and reuniting in him each and every man, every human value."[2] Each of those verbs is significant in Congar's definition. The function of the church is to assimilate. It is the very opposite of a closed, self-contained society; she must constantly be nourished by what is outside her own communion. Yet she cannot swallow anything whole. She must bring her own spirit to discern and purify, to fecundate what is sterile and to foster what has promise and thus to fulfill. And always her action must be vertical as well as horizontal. It is only because she is drawn by God that she can penetrate and elevate humanity outside her boundaries. There is here no humanitarian parliament, no purely human give and take between various opinions. The sole hope for human unification through the church rests upon utter obedience to God.

There is a danger of conceiving catholicity too abstractly. The faith of the Bible does not gather concrete particulars under a universal principle. Quite the contrary. It is particular, flesh and blood reality under which universal principles are gathered. The catholicity of the church is not a philosophical truth, a unity of many different groups in some over-arching idea. Israel, as God's people in the Old Testament, is no abstraction but an historical people. Indeed the unity of Israel in some common vision of life is far less evident than her unity as one people with a common historical destiny. Similarly the unity of the Christian church is not to be sought primarily in the realm of ideas but on the level of real human beings in all their often distressing particularity. The center of the Christian church is Jesus himself, not his teaching alone but deeper still his very person, and so the church is catholic first of all not because she gathers many people under one set of teachings, but because Jesus is risen and alive and many men and women are united with him in a vital community of faith, hope and love. The church is the "new Israel," the people of God. Her bonds are not only those of beautiful ideals but the far more ambiguous and yet more fully human ties that join living human beings with each other in a common task.

Let us set down as plainly and simply as possible the essence of Christian belief in the catholicity of the church. Jesus Christ came to save *all* men. There are few assertions more centrally rooted in Christian faith than this. From Peter's forceful words in the *Acts of the Apostles*, "There is salvation in no one else {than Jesus}, for there is no other name under heaven given to men by which we must be saved,"[5] through Paul's many ways of asserting that "no one is justified by works of the Law but through faith in Jesus Christ"[6] and down through the centuries of Christian tradition, Christians have clung stubbornly to this universal claim, in spite of all difficulties. It has been a bone of contention to other religions and an embarrassment to many Christians. It would be so much easier and so much more acceptable to others to say that Jesus offers one way to salvation among many others. But this would be to abandon a large part of the New Testament and to sacrifice a truth that lies at the heart of Christian faith.

What Christians have believed, they have also practiced. The sense of a universal mission, of being sent to all mankind has driven men and women to every continent and to every class of people. It has been stronger than danger and torture and privation. Christians have never been willing to accept a "sphere of influence" theory, comparable to that which has prevailed in world politics. They have refused to acknowledge that any nation, race or class was out of bounds, where their message was at stake. Francis Xavier dying in the attempt to penetrate the forbidden kingdom of China and worker-priests struggling to bring the gospel to a de-Christianized society are living testimonials to the faith that Christ came for all.

Earlier generations have understood the universal Christian mission in a simpler, less complicated way than is possible for us. It is scarcely possible to hold that all mankind is called to actual, explicit membership in the Christian community, in the light of what we know now about the age of humanity and the fact of whole civilizations which came and went without any discoverable contact with historical Christianity. Surely the universal mission of the Christian church must be conceived in terms of a service rendered to multitudes who remain outside her visible communion. Recent reflection on the nature of mission has lead to a more deeply "catholic" understanding than was possible to a sixteenth century apostle like Francis Xavier, but let us bypass the exact nature of the universal mission of Christ for the moment. Our purpose here is only to recall the audacious claim at the heart of Christian faith that the grace of Christ is for all. The Spirit, who burst upon the earliest believers as a consequence of Christ's death and resurrection, drove them out of the little upper room in Jerusalem "even to the ends of the earth" and symbolically equipped them with the gift of tongues to deliver them from every barrier of language and culture which might have confined their message to any segment of humanity.

Sensitive and contentious as that universalist claim is, it does respond to a critical need of our secular world today, the need for human unity in a world too small to survive without it. If the pathways to God are permanently and necessarily divided, then the secular dream of world unity so cherished by thoughtful people at present, whatever their religious position, depends exclusively on humanistic resources for its realization. But if Jesus Christ is truly unique with an indispensable role to play in the destiny of all mankind, and has come "to gather into one all the scattered children of God"[7] then the secular dream of unity is confirmed and sustained at the deepest level of human motivation—the religious level. World unity is a divine as well as a human project and human efforts to achieve the kind of cooperation between nations, races and groups which appears more impossible than ever to attain, while at the same time more desperately necessary, can enlist the support of religious faith. Our contemporary world could use such support. Of course the fact that it would be good for us if the Christian claims were true does not make them true, but it does at least make them interesting, and if any promise is timely in our contemporary situation, quite apart from religious faith, it is that which offers hope for the unification of mankind.

What we have been describing might be called geographical or horizontal catholicity; it is a movement outward in space, the diffusion of what God made present in Jerusalem to all places and peoples. Seen in this light alone, catholicity is a one-way street. But God's revelation is not a monologue. It is the first step in a dialogue between God and the human family. It calls for a response. God's grace is a power that brings to life, not a packaged gift which is received passively. It awakens what is already within us, individually and socially, sets us in motion and begins a partnership in which our resources are energized and directed by God's Holy Spirit. Consequently what each person and each culture brings to God's work is distinctive, and the product of collaboration with God will be distinctive as well. The fabric the Holy Spirit is weaving through the centuries is a coat of many colors. Perhaps we have been too individualistic and pietistic in our viewpoint to appreciate the great variety which is possible in the church of God. If our unity with Christ touched only our personal, interior life, the range for diversity would be large enough, but when we realize that it is the whole of our society and our culture which is to be brought to Christ, the possibilities expand immeasurably. St. Paul pointed out more than once the great diversity of gifts the Holy Spirit bestowed upon the church and he adds that all of these are given "to equip God's people for work in his service, to the building up of the body of Christ. So shall we all attain to the unity inherent in our faith and our knowledge of the Son of God—to mature manhood, measured by nothing less than the full stature of Christ."[8] Paul is not thinking here about individual Christians alone, because he concludes with a marvelous expression of the function of diverse but unified members in the social body of the church,

...so shall we fully grow up into Christ. He is the head, and on him, the whole body depends. Bonded and knit together by every constituent joint, the whole frame grows through the due activity of each part, and builds itself up in love.[9]

Let me illustrate what I am driving at. Every culture rests upon a certain vision of life as a whole. This overall vision produces a unique and distinctive pattern of existence; out of it arise the institutions, practices, art, music, etc. which constitute the culture. Some values will be cherished more than others, some virtues will be more evident than others. Countless factors, environmental, historical, psychological produce this distinctive pattern over time and conversely the peculiar shape of life produced will condition and mold the viewpoints, the sensitivities of those whose culture it is, resulting in a distinctive human experience with no exact parallel anywhere in history. The vision of life is neither sterile nor static. It is not sterile because it shapes the ways of acting and it is not static because those ways of acting flow back upon the world view which shaped them, modifying it in the light of experience. If this is true then the world view which comes from Christ and his followers will not emerge unchanged from contact with different cultures anymore than the newly penetrated cultures will be unaffected by Christianity.

Take the American Indians, for example (if it is possible to generalize about one such culture in spite of the great diversity of different tribes). They have developed a way of relating to the environment, a pattern of human relationships, a harmony with the forces of nature, a philosophy of life and death, which differentiates them from the European peoples who received Christianity before them. Evidently the Christian church will be enriched the more this culture is assimilated—critically of course—as the Indian culture will gain immeasurably from contact with the historical heritage of Jesus and his church.

If what we have called geographical or horizontal catholicity were the whole story, the process of conversion would be complete once all the members of a tribe had been baptized, provision had been made for the Eucharist to be celebrated and the Sacraments to be administered and the catechism to be translated from a European language into the local tongue. Patterns of family life within the tribe would remain unchanged, images of God would be the same although a new name would be substituted for the old. Obviously there is more to conversion than this. The Christian message would have to penetrate more deeply (vertically) into the Indian culture. Ways of dealing with sexuality, of raising children, of treating hostile tribes, expectations from heavenly beings, all would have to be challenged with the gospel of Jesus, and on the other hand, the Indians' awareness of the presence of God in nature, their profound stories and symbols of the invisible world would break open some narrow and static viewpoints of the missionaries. Ideally a new *kind* of Christianity would be the product (not totally new, of course, but new in significant respects).

Isn't it logical to say that as long as any nation, race or civilization has not made its own peculiar and irreplaceable contribution to the saving work of Christ, then the growth of the church, which is Christ's body is stunted; it has not reached full maturity, and is not as catholic as it could be? Of course we cannot presume to know the details of God's plan. The mystery of freedom requires that the possibility of refusal and incompleteness remain a part of the plan, and we dare not apply our measure of perfection to the inscrutable designs of God. But we can recognize that catholicity is an endless task, one that will not be fully accomplished before Jesus comes again.

Conversion is a matter of degrees; it is the task of a lifetime to deepen our faith and to grow in the likeness of Jesus. But this is only to concentrate on the individual believer; once we expand our horizon to the society and culture of which the individual is a part—and as never before we are aware of how inseparable each individual is from his or her society—the space to be permeated by the gospel stretches out indefinitely. How disturbing it is to observe in two thousand years of history how often Christians have followed patterns of culture which were thoroughly alien to the gospel of Jesus Christ! Too often their fault has been deliberate and blameworthy, oftener still they have been unaware of the implications of their faith. God's revelation does not come full blown upon humanity. It has taken many centuries to draw out some of its implications and who would dare to say that the process is near completion! We read in the Old Testament of the savagery of God's people toward their enemies and this performed in the name of God and with full confidence in his approval. Only those will be scandalized who fail to realize that God takes people as they are and only gradually draws them to a purer understanding of his will. We see the intolerance, superstition and bigotry, that has defiled Christian conduct through the centuries, but the same principle is at work. What we have here is cultural remains which have never been subjugated to Christian faith, assumptions that have never been tested in the spirit of the gospel, customs carried over from paganism, ancient and modern, which have never been baptized, or perhaps have only been baptized externally, remaining untouched in their inner core by the word of God. We are, all of us, the products of our civilization; we accept the myths, the values, the patterns of living common to our society, unless a prophet arises to show us a better way, and even then it takes a long time for that prophetic light to penetrate. Gradual development is the norm in moral as well as in physical reality. The individualism and privatization of religion so widespread in the nineteenth century have obscured our vision, but in fact souls cannot be saved apart from living human beings and human beings cannot be saved in isolation from each other and from the culture which permeates their being even in its most spiritual moments. Unless the saving power of the Holy Spirit reaches into the structures of society, structures of thought and structures of action, the building blocks of actual human existence, the kingdom of God will be thin and ethereal indeed.

On the other hand the absence of this wider catholicity is perhaps the most serious problem facing the church today. Peter Berger, in his writings on religious sociology, has referred to the "cognitive dissonance" which threatens Christians at present.[10] What this means is that all of us think and judge instinctively according to the accepted patterns of our society. When those patterns are in conflict with the vision of Christian faith, a painful tension arises for believers. Some such tension is intrinsic to Christian faith at all times, but the discordance can reach such a pitch of intensity that it is almost impossible for believers to survive both as members of the wider society they share with their non-believing contemporaries and also as members of the community of faith. When such a situation occurs, one allegiance will be sacrificed for the sake of the other. Either believers will form a closed community of their own, after the fashion of the Essenes of the first century and numerous others since then, or the substance of faith will be dissolved into the prevailing world-view, retaining, perhaps, the language and rituals of the old faith, but abandoning it in fact.

There is, however, a third possibility. Christian faith can be brought into vital contact with the contemporary civilization in genuine but critical fidelity to both. Neither the total cultural package of believers, as it existed in the past, nor the whole contemporary civilization will survive intact. Both will change but what is genuinely valuable in each will remain. The task of reconciling the two is what we mean by catholicity in the wider sense.

Catholic or catholic?

Common nouns and adjectives have a way of turning into proper nouns, and once they do, their connection with the original meaning often weakens or is even completely lost. Probably the first men called Smith got their name because they made their living shoeing horses but few of their modern descendants follow the same trade. The great biblical names, Abraham, Samuel, Joshua, etc. were given to individuals because the name described who they were and what task they were to accomplish, but we use the same names today with little thought for their original meaning. The Pilgrims set aside a special holiday to give thanks to God for his blessings, but it is safe to say that our modern "Thanksgiving Day" has only a tenuous connection with the religious sentiment on which it was founded. The "catholic" character of the Church, which we have just described at some length, has become the proper name of one large group of Christians. Has it suffered the same fate as many other words with their own meaning, once they have been changed into a proper noun? Is the connection between the Catholic Church (capitalized) and the catholicity of the Church of Christ only an historical memory? My answer as a Roman Catholic is, of course, "No."

It may be well in passing to acknowledge that what is said on this particular point represents the distinct theological perspective of a Roman Catholic, whereas little else in this book derives from a peculiarly or exclusively Catholic point of view. Even here, allowing for some ambiguity in the understanding of the expression "Catholic Church," I suspect that most Christian theologians belonging to other communions would find little to disagree with.

It is true that in the nineteenth and early twentieth century, Catholics—and especially American Catholics—were more sectarian and consequently less "catholic" than most of their fellow Christians, but if you look beyond the concrete situation of Catholics in the nineteenth century, which was after all the product of particular and by no means typical historical circumstances, to the official teaching and the age-old traditions of the Church of Rome, you will find much evidence of commitment to universality and a refusal of particularism and sectarianism. Obviously this cannot be said of every official document or every decision, but I would be prepared to argue that nothing has been more characteristic of the Church of Rome even empirically than her consciousness of a mission to all mankind, her openness to all cultures and her eagerness to assimilate their diverse values, coupled with a reluctance to close any doors or exclude anything, whether it be ideas, customs or human institutions of any sort, as long as a possibility of accommodation and conversion remained. Indeed this avidity for adaptation and adoption has been the source of weakness as well as strength within the Church of Rome, weakness which has called forth necessary protests on the part of other Christians with a stricter understanding of the demands of the gospel, but the point here is not to evaluate but only to affirm the catholicity of the Catholic tradition. The unravelling of Christian unity during the sixteenth century and even more the collapse of the social structures of the Middle Ages, in the face of triumphant secularism in the nineteenth century, produced a defensiveness among Catholics which was unfriendly to the "catholic" spirit. Added to this in America, the requirements for survival in a hostile environment prodded Catholics into the "ghetto" mentality of the recent past, but there is every sign that the defensive atmosphere of the past few centuries is being blown away by the winds of the late twentieth century.

The Second Vatican Council was the dramatic climax of a process of reversing the defensiveness and isolation of the nineteenth century and of opening out to other Christians in the documents on the church and on ecumenism, to other religions in the declaration on the relation of the church to non-Christian religions and to the whole secular world in the pastoral constitution on the church in the modern world, to single out only the most notable examples. Progressives within the Catholic Church have been alarmed at a restrictive tendency at work in official church circles more recently, but the special synod call in 1985 to evaluate the outcome of the council some twenty years after it ended, demonstrates that the main lines of reform legislated by the council are solidly and lastingly in place.

Perhaps it would be well to spell out in some detail the relation between the Catholic Church and the quality of being catholic as an attribute of Christ's church, as this relation appears to Roman Catholic theology. First of all, it is important to insist that the church of Christ is not an abstraction but an historical reality. As we pointed out before, Judaeo-Christian faith is incorrigibly concrete. Any attempt to reduce the religion of either the New or the Old Testament to a "wisdom," an insight into the nature of existence or any series of teachings, however profound, must conflict with the most distinctive feature of the Bible, namely that it relates a sacred *history*. It is concerned with what God has *done*, not only what he has explained. Its content is less in the domain of ideas than in actual events and institutions, the things about which history is written, but which in the domain of ideas are often poorly understood. The distinction is subtle, perhaps, but crucial. When Jews at a Seder meal and Christians at the Eucharist give expression to their faith, it is the great *deeds* of God not just his words that they recite. According to the Second Vatican Council revelation is comprised of "deeds and words having an inner unity: the deeds wrought by God in the history of salvation manifest and confirm the teaching and realities signified by the words, while the words proclaim the deeds and clarify the mystery contained in them."[9] Neither the words of the Bible taken by themselves, therefore, nor the events to which they refer constitute God's revelation. Both are necessary and one depends upon the other. Revelation cannot be reduced to words or ideas. Christian faith is not just an interpretation of common human experience, not just another "symbol-system" for making sense of the experience common to all humanity. The experience as well as its interpretation is special and unique. God has *done* something in Jesus Christ.

Against the background of a belief that God is the creator of all that is and his providence extends to all mankind, Judaeo-Christian faith stands or falls on the conviction that God has entered into a new and special partnership or covenant with Israel. God has entered human history, this world of living, breathing human beings with their wars and their rivalries, their earthly ambitions and their failures, not just as a teacher, who offers advice from outside, from the safety of Heaven, but as a participant, Emmanuel—God with us. This he has done in the events of Israel's history. This he has done supremely, in an altogether unexpected way, in the Person of Jesus, who is not only the messenger of God, delivering God's teaching, but, according to the shattering affirmation of orthodox faith, who is himself God in person, God become man, the Word made flesh. It has always been extremely difficult to accept such a "hard saying" and many Christians have gone away from it into some form of Gnosticism to minimize the scandal of so mind-boggling a doctrine. Perhaps today more than ever in the radical questioning of our time, Christians are tempted to reduce the shocking truth of the Incarnation to the more manageable demands of a pure myth or symbol, which our contemporaries would find easier to accept, but the orthodox faith of Christianity stands in the way of any such accommodation.

In application to our present subject this requires that we put aside any notion of an invisible Church of Christ, which would possess the quality of catholicity, being endowed with some completely spiritual or intellectual unity, in contrast with all visible churches, which can be no more than sects of Christians, as irreconcilable with the historical character of Judaeo-Christian faith. It is not an invisible, purely spiritual unity to which God is summoning the human family, according to the Bible, but a fully human communion, which must include visible, structural elements, without which human community and human collaboration in a common task is impossible. The model for the desired unity of mankind with God and with each other is not the unity of many men and women in a common ideal but the unity of God and man in the flesh of Jesus Christ. Catholics are not willing to exclude from the Church of Christ the visible structures by which the human community of Christians is organized, nor do they consider these structures as accidental and arbitrary. The fact that the structural elements of the Church, which Catholics consider essential, include structures of authority such as episcopate and papacy is one of the few remaining barriers to ecumenical unity. On the other hand, to defend the institutional and governmental elements as belonging by right to the Church of Christ is not to propose that they are the only or the most important ingredients in the community, nor to deny that such elements can assume widely different forms as far as their method of operation is concerned.

In sum, then, we can say that Roman Catholics insist on the genuinely human and historical character of the Christian Church. The Church of Christ is present in this world, very imperfectly indeed, but truly; she looks forward to a harvest time when the seed which has been planted will be fully grown and the weeds so evident in the present, will be gone, nonetheless, even in her present, historical reality she is the Body of Christ and the instrument of the Holy Spirit, and those qualities which belong to his church because he is present there, making her one, holy, catholic and apostolic, belong to the church in history, to the very human community bound together, as every community must be, by visible, structural bonds. These qualities exist in very rudimentary form now, but they have taken root and are growing. For a Catholic theologian there cannot be a sharp distinction between Catholic, written with a capital letter, and catholic, as an adjective describing the whole church of Christ. He must settle for some ambiguity. Catholicity as an attribute of the church according to the creeds common to most Christians is a summons to the unity not of an abstract idea but to the unity of one flock and one shepherd, to the unity expressed by a proper noun, the unity of one historical community, in which people are joined to each other by all the visible, organizational and institutional bonds, which are necessary for any group of men and women to live and work together. The catholicity of Christianity calls for a Catholic Church.

However uncomfortable it makes them from an ecumenical point of view, Catholic theologians cannot deny that according to their faith the Catholic Church is not one more among many Christian sects. It has always made a universal claim. Such expressions as "Outside the Church, there is no salvation" can hardly be understood today in the naively simple way medievals could understand them, with an image of the world extending not far beyond the Mediterranean basin and an image of human history limited to two or three millennia, not to mention an insensitivity to many psychological and sociological factors affecting human choice, which modern research has uncovered. The official voice of the Church no less than the Christian theological community in general has repudiated any notion that eternal salvation is limited to those who explicitly profess the Christian creed and are counted as formal members of the Catholic community and it would be well to disassociate completely such a naive interpretation from the universalist claims of the Catholic Church. The catholicity we affirm of the church in the Nicene creed does not rest upon such a fundamentalist reading of the Scriptures. Yet the universalist claim still stands, deeply rooted in the core of faith that Jesus is the savior of all mankind, the alpha and omega of human history, and that the salvation he offers is not a private experience which takes place entirely within the limits of personal consciousness, but citizenship within a kingdom of God and sharing in a community of love.

Two Ways of Defining the Church

The universalist claim of the Catholic Church is intelligible only if we are prepared to define the "Catholic Church" in a way unacceptable to non-believers and a way which usually makes believers also uncomfortable in our statistically minded age. Let me suggest two different but not mutually exclusive definitions of the Catholic Church. In the first case the Catholic Church can be described empirically, on the basis of elements which are externally verifiable. As such, the Catholic church is a human grouping like any other. It has a "constitution" and laws like any state or society; it has officials and patterns of governance, its members can be counted in a census; it has gatherings and ceremonies, customs and traditions. To define the Catholic Church in this way requires no judgement of faith; it would be possible to agree on such a definition, whatever one's opinion about the value of such a society. On the other hand, the believer can accept such a definition as true but incomplete, leaving out what in the believer's view is most important but accurate as far as it goes. Such a definition I propose to call "the Catholic Church looked at sociologically." This kind of definition, supposing it is carefully drawn up, identifies the Catholic Church in so far as it can be known by the techniques of empirical science or as it would appear to a professional sociologist, whose only concern was to describe accurately the human grouping known as the Catholic Church, without presuppositions regarding the truth or falsehood of its own self image.

Yet such a definition falls infinitely short of the real church of Jesus Christ as she has appeared to Christian faith since the earliest days of her existence. To pursue an analogy from the constitution on the Church in the Second Vatican Council, many of those who made contact with Jesus during his ministry in Israel saw only a man like any other. The disciples who formed the core of the Christian church would not have denied what the others saw. It was true as far as it went, but they would have insisted that the Holy Spirit gave the power to see much more, to see what "flesh and blood" could not perceive. This man was the "only begotten Son of God." Similarly, unbelievers of later ages can recognize the Catholic Church; if they have a sophisticated command of social science, they can identify the social dynamics which control its operations, but the believing Christian will never agree that this is the whole story. He is convinced that this real, concrete community in all its humanness, made up of all the elements found in any society of real human beings, is also a mystery of faith. It can be described by the many metaphores of the New Testament. It is the new Israel, the kingdom of God, the body of Christ, the true vine, the temple of living stones, the bride of Christ, the dwelling place of the Holy Spirit. At its center is not the record of Christ's words and deeds, but the living, risen Jesus himself. Its radical source of energy and direction is not a governmental structure, which can be plotted on a managerial chart, but the Holy Spirit.

This second definition of the church I would like to call the "Catholic Church looked at theologically," that is as seen within the context of faith. If this vision of faith is true, the Catholic Church is incomparably bigger than it appears externally; its resources and its methods of operating are not limited to those of other human groups. In every direction it bursts the bonds of its visible components. It is not that the visible elements are cancelled out by the spiritual—and I use the word *spiritual* here not in its general sense but in its properly Christian sense as coming from the Holy

Spirit—but they are only part of a larger whole. The paradox of the church, as of her founder, is the marriage of visible and invisible, human and divine.

Terminology is going to a problem throughout this book, but perhaps we are in a position now to state clearly how we see the relation between Catholic and catholic. Only for the Catholic Church looked at theologically can the universal claim be made. To identify the Catholic Church looked at sociologically with the catholic character of Christian would be intolerably narrow and hardly credible in our times. It is only because the visible reality of the Christian church is like the tip of a great iceberg that we can assert that she is sent to all men and that all are called to her company. The Second Vatican Council in its constitution on the church took a giant step forward, as far as Roman Catholic theology is concerned, when it said in a sentence, rich in its ecumenical implications, that the one and only Church of Christ, which is called one, holy, catholic and apostolic, in the creeds, "subsists in the Catholic Church, governed by the successor of Peter and the Bishops in communion with him, although outside of its boundaries there exist many elements of sanctification and truth, which as gifts proper to Christ's Church lead to catholic unity."[12] The word "subsists" is significant. It does not affirm complete identity between the Catholic Church looked at theologically and the Catholic Church looked at sociologically, after the fashion of an earlier, counter-Reformation apologetics and it recognizes explicitly that the former is far more extensive than the latter. On the other hand, it does not cut off the true Church of Jesus Christ from the struggling historical community of his disciples, where the Spirit is already at work not only within the souls of individual believers but also through the flawed instrumentality of the community itself.

Throughout the chapters to follow we will often use the word "catholic" and frequently it will not be clear which of the two definitions proposed above is at issue. Is it the historical church which calls itself Catholic or the wider, less tangible reality, which extends much beyond the bounds of the historical community? The ambiguity must remain. Clarity is not always a virtue, especially when it can only be achieved at the price of an impoverished image of a reality too rich for our words and concepts. Those accustomed to scientific method are impatient when language is less exact, but anyone who would think or speak of God and of his works must settle for some measure of mystery.

Notes

1. For a thorough historical study of CATHOLICITY and a more scholarly and theological analysis of its many aspects than is attempted in these pages, the reader should consult the recent work of Avery Dulles, *The Catholicity Of The Church* (N.Y.: Oxford University Press, 1985).

2. 1 Peter 3:15.

3. *Catholicism: A Study Of Dogma In Relation To The Corporate Destiny Of Mankind,* trans. Lancelot C. Sheppard, a Mentor-Omega book, (N.Y.: The New American Library of World Literature, 1964).

4. *Chretiens Desunis* (Paris: Editions du cerf, 1937) p. 177.

5. Acts 4:12.

6. Gal. 2:16

7. Jn. 11:52

8. Eph. 4:12, 13 (New English Bible translation). We have tried to use inclusive language throughout this book, however, in sections where anthropological questions are considered at length, the word "man" is sometimes used in a generic sense, for want of a better term and to avoid wordiness.

9. Eph. 4:15,16.

10. of. "Secular Theology and the Rejection of the Supernatural: Reflections on Recent Trends," *Theological Studies,* Vol.38 (March,1977), pp. 39-58. See also *A Rumor Of Angels* (Garden City, N.Y.: Anchor Books, Doubleday, 1970), Chapter 1.

11. *Documents Of Vatican Two, Dogmatic Constitution On Divine Revelation* (Dei Verbum), trans. Walter M. Abbott, No. 2.

12. Ibid, *Dogmatic Constitution On The Church (Lumen Gentium),* No. 8.

Chapter Two

Only a Community Can Be Catholic

Let me state the argument of this chapter as boldly as possible first of all, recognizing that many qualifications are called for and will be provided as we proceed. We can only think, live and pray in *community*. The isolated individual is an illusion. Whether we are aware of it or not, it is the community which thinks in us and acts in us, as well as we in the community. Even when we are rebelling against it, the community is at work in us. There is simply no way of separating ourselves completely from the communities to which we belong, even in our most private moments. The fact that we have learned this so thoroughly in recent times is one reason why the Christian church is summoned today as never before in history to appreciate its catholicity. Catholicity is essentially a community virtue and only a community can truly be catholic.

It may be important to clear away some of the associations of that word "community." I am using the word in its widest sense. Any group of people who have *anything* in common form a community (common-ity), as the word is used in this chapter. Readers may think instinctively about "community drives" and "community agencies." The accent is on external collaboration and perhaps relatively superficial activities. One of the purposes of this chapter is to refute just such an understanding of community, which, I suspect, is itself the product of excessive individualism and privatization. Not only external and legalistic goods are common but also internal and spiritual ones. "Community" as we are talking about it in this chapter is opposed only to individualism, to the illusion that persons are fully constituted in themselves and depend on others only for external and superficial needs.

It was easier a century or two ago for a person to think of herself or himself in a highly individualistic fashion, as one who thought for himself, made his own decisions, was totally "objective," refusing any influence from inherited or acquired prejudices. His intellectual ideal was the "scientific method," which put him in contact with reality pure and simple, unaffected by any superstition. Myth and metaphysics could be consigned to an unenlightened past; they served no useful purpose for modern man. His plans and decisions were founded on pragmatic considerations, on statistics and scientific data, rather than on tradition in any form. Today such a picture of human conduct could scarcely be defended with intellectual honesty. If there is one thing that modern psychology and philosophy have taught us it is that we never touch being in pure objectivity but only in so far as we are in subjective contact with it, and what is more to the point here, we bring to every experience a heavy baggage of expectations deriving from past experience, individual and social. The social groups to which we belong have marked us and shaped our perception of the world both by the heritage which comes through our genes and by the cultural heritage which has formed our way of thinking and feeling. The dependence is not total, of course. We can and should be critical, and the more deeply we penetrate our human inheritance the more critical we can be, but our most critical evaluation will come from within that inheritance not from some Archimedean point cut adrift from all social moorings. There is no such thing as unadulterated objectivity. Every vision is from a particular point of view and that point of view is never purely individual.

There is an historical ingredient to every fragment of human knowledge, which is to say that it is only known by one who stands within history and in the way it can be known from that particular standpoint in history. To stand within history is to be influenced by those who have gone before and by those who share the same moment in time and place.

Are we arguing here for total determinism? Not at all. For one thing all of us belong not to one but to many communities and the interaction between these many communities offers a wide scope for freedom. Even within the same community many ways of belonging are possible. Yet sometimes those who are most anxious to vindicate freedom for themselves and others seem to identify freedom with utter individualism. They feel that to be free means to be guided exclusively by oneself, to suffer no influence from others. But surely this is an adolescent notion of freedom and one far removed from the actuality of human existence. Human freedom need not be defended at the expense of realism. To be free is not to be unaffected and uninfluenced by others; it is rather to choose among influences. The rugged individualist whose choices are strictly and exclusively his own is a figment of the imagination. Man has no choice as to whether he will form part of a community in his internal as well as his external acts; there is no alternative. His only choice is whether he will do so consciously and selectively or without awareness.

Another way of saying all of this is that man is inescapably social in every dimension of his or her being, in religion and values as well as in habits of eating and dressing. Put in such abstract terms, this is hardly a new discovery. What is new is the concrete evidence from every branch of knowledge which has translated this philosophical truth into a matter of detailed observation. It was possible in the Middle Ages to conceive of human knowledge as little more than a reflection of the external world, as though our senses and, in a more spiritual way, our intellects, were a kind of mirror on which the image of external reality was impressed.[1] From such a perspective the individual has a more direct grip upon the world beyond himself than that any educated modern can claim. Since Emmanuel Kant such naive realism and the individualistic understanding of knowledge that could be joined to it have become impossible. To know is not to receive the impress of some external object upon our internal faculties, but an intense interaction between a subject knowing and an object known, in which subjective and objective aspects are inseparably mingled. What we bring to knowledge is as important as what we receive and what we bring is social or at least it is something which comes from beyond ourselves. The way we know anything is by applying to it structures, images, concepts and language, which are not of our own manufacture but which we have inherited from others, however this heritage is transmitted. Human knowledge is social not individualistic. The knowledge we have of external reality is always mediated by and in a community. Even that activity which seems most individual and which provides the foundation for individual choice is itself a community project. In a true sense we can only think within community.

Confirmation from Psychology

Let me suggest a few areas of modern research which have underlined the social character of human experience at its highest levels, that is, where it is concerned with religion, morality and value.

First, there is the new awareness of subconscious and unconscious factors in human conduct, which dates from Sigmund Freud. To confine our understanding of ourselves and others to those reasons and motives of which we are fully conscious is to leave out of consideration great depths of our own psychic reality. It is a prescription for the most incurable deception of all—self-deception. Those who are supremely confident of their own interpretation of the Bible, for example, risk being the victims of irrational forces lodged too deeply in their own *psyche* to be drawn out by ordinary discourse. The arguments from the Bible, which, as they see it, have persuaded them to a certain pattern of conduct, may not be the real reason why they are acting in this way. They may be rationalizations rather than genuine reasons. What may be expressing itself in their lives could be some psychic wound received in the past but now buried beyond the power of recall. This may be the most insidious social influence of all, insidious because others who may have wounded us however indeliberately in the past are still controlling our conduct in the present, even when we are convinced that we are doing so ourselves.

The catholic spirit offers some protection against this tyranny of individual conscience. It opens us to influences wider than our own personal resources and even those of our own limited group and it alerts us to the possibility of self deception. True, it provides no simple formula for balancing the claims of individual conscience and those of the larger community. Christian history offers too many examples of saints who have been called to follow a lonely path against the pressures of the community to conclude that the eccentric or the prophetic figure is regularly deluded. Still, the fault is not always on the side of the community. There has been enough fanaticism and intolerance on the part of Christians convinced of a divine call to point up the ambiguity of the problem. There is no easy way to distinguish a true, personal vocation from pathological drives that can counterfeit God's grace, but it remains true that an open Christian community is the best protection against the subterranean forces, of which Freudian psychology has made us aware. The individual is situated against a wider background; one which includes not only the wisdom and good sense of men but the Word of God in many forms and the history of his dealings with the human family through many centuries. The result may not be an infallible discernment of the voice of God in particular cases but it is a great help. In any case the discovery of the subconscious has underlined the social character of human knowledge.

This is especially true if we turn to more recent psychologists, who have followed in the path of Freud but with an ear more attuned to social factors. Freud was preoccupied with individual needs, that for security and affection especially, but Erich Fromm among others has shown how inadequate the fulfillment of such personal needs proves to be. At least as fundamental as our need for pleasure is our need "to belong," to be part of a whole greater than ourselves, to see our own lives in a context of meaning, of community. When this need goes unsatisfied no amount of physical pleasure or material abundance brings happiness. Fromm has traced the growth of totalitarianism in our century to just such an absence.[2] If men and women cannot relate to each other in love, in true human community, they will turn to subhuman forms of association based on force and violence to fill the painful vacuum. Evidently this finding of psychology echoes the gospel of Jesus Christ and thereby suggests something more profound about human existence than psychology is aware of, but I call attention to it here only because it demonstrates the inadequacy of individualism on every level and shows that human existence is social to its very core.

The failure of individualism is that it is preoccupied with the conscious life of the individual person. As we have seen, Freudian psychology has expanded that horizon by showing that this conscious level on which we make rational decisions is only the surface of a greater continent, even of personal experience. Carl Jung has gone further. He has discovered that the make-up of that hidden continent is not just our own individual experience but the memory of the race. In our own subconscious we are in contact with generations of our ancestors. Buried there are symbols or archetypes of human experience much wider than our own. The meaning of these symbols is not arbitrary; in part at least, it comes to us already fashioned by our ancestors. Our psychic experience is a communion with humanity even when we are most alone, in our dreams and our fantasies.

From the viewpoint of an earlier, more individualistic and rationalistic age, we would expect that people could create their own symbols and assign them whatever meaning they wished, after the fashion of algebraic symbols. If our image of humanity is centered too exclusively on the rational powers of the individual human being, that is what we would expect, but what anthropologists and psychologists have discovered does not correspond to this expectation. Symbols are not purely arbitrary; they have a structure and consistency of their own; they cut across cultures and religions, not totally, of course, but enough to undermine the individualistic and rationalistic assumptions we mentioned above.

The extensive research that has been done in comparative religion in the last century is pertinent here. It has exposed so much that is common to widely scattered religious traditions. On the surface one religion seems totally different from others but the more we penetrate beneath the surface the more they seem to converge, the more we discover of common insights into the human condition and even common symbols. It would be wrong to exaggerate because study also brings to light subtle but profound differences that escape superficial observers, but this convergence of different religions creates an anguishing temptation for Christians. There is no escaping the fact that Christianity makes claim to originality and uniqueness. It can never see itself as just a different way of expressing a wisdom common to all humanity. In its own eyes Christianity is the record of a unique intervention of God into human history, one which concerns all humanity, not because it expresses in a particularly helpful way what can be known in many other ways, but because the one event which it records is a world event in which all are called to participate. But if Christians must defend the originality and uniqueness of their faith—as indeed they must—it cannot be done in the simple, uncomplicated way that was possible some centuries ago. The rediscovery of Semitic civilizations by archaeologists has shown that there was much in common between the religious world of the Old Testament and that of their pagan neighbors. To take one example, the story of Job has parallels in the literature of many peoples other than Israel so it seems likely that the inspired author of that Old Testament book did not derive his material directly and exclusively from Israelite sources but was content to use a well-known tale and to shape it according to the distinctive vision of God's people. Many of the psalms, too, borrow in large part from songs, prayers, folklore and images of the surrounding nations. Similarly when it comes to the New Testament, the fuller knowledge of Greco-Roman civilization of the first century has revealed how much Christians adopted from their neighbors, and even more how much common elements within the Mediterranean culture surfaced both in the experience of the early Christians and in other contemporary movements. Earlier generations could picture the church in her infancy as modelled on detailed instructions given by Jesus himself, but it is clear now that no such detailed instructions were available to the apostles and their successors and so they did not hesitate to use Jewish and secular models they were familiar with to organize their communities, determine the responsibilities of various officials, structure their rituals, etc. The essentials of church order do derive from the time of Jesus' ministry and the post-resurrection experience of the apostles, but these essentials are much less precise and detailed than authors of the sixteenth century, for example, imagined.

Two interpretations of this new information are possible: either one can renounce the distinctive claims of biblical faith and watch the Christian religion be swallowed up in humanism, or one can see striking new evidence of the catholic character of Christian faith. It is the second route we choose to follow. The uniqueness of Christianity is not that it has sprung full blown from heaven to become the exclusive property of one limited segment of humanity, but that it reaches into the depths of man's social nature and makes contact with the common grounds of all human experience. Its genius is not to reject the common symbols and universal longings and intimations of the human family; in order to substitute something totally new and different, but to gather up and unify in the person of Jesus what is scattered everywhere and to direct what is already common into the greater community of the kingdom of God.

Language Is a Function of Community

Related to what we have just been discussing but extending beyond it in many directions is the whole field of reflection on language which has received so much attention from philosophers and anthropologists in recent times. Language is a function of community. Whenever we use language, whether in our most private reflections or in conversation with others, the community is at work in us. For this most personal of human experiences, where we develop and express what is most peculiarly and uniquely our own, we are dependent upon a social instrument. "Language" is susceptible to a wide range of meanings, of course, and we use the term in its widest extension, but whatever the language involved, that of ordinary words or bodily gestures or in any other form, it is the community not the individual alone which creates it and only the community can interpret it.

Those who have not had occasion to deal with more than one language—using the word here in its most obvious sense, e.g., English, French, Latin, etc.—are usually unaware of the complexities of translation. Suppose, for example, we wish to translate from Greek into English. The uninitiated readily think of three different things: first, a common set of objects—trees, buildings, political institutions—second, a Greek set of labels for these objects and finally a parallel English set of labels for the same common objects of experience. The translator's job would then be simply to exchange English labels for their Greek equivalents. It is one of the merits of exposure to another language and another civilization to be quickly disabused of any such understanding. There is no common set of objects. The Greek experience of the world has been very different from that of English speaking people and their different way of relating to it and understanding it comes to expression in their language. The natural environment may be similar, though even the word "tree" (in whatever language) does not refer to exactly the same reality when it is spoken by people living in a desert as it does when spoken in the topics, but the political and cultural institutions of people living in Greek city-states, relatively isolated even from their contemporaries a thousand miles away and unaffected by the rise of Christianity and the whole array of modern technology and communications have no exact parallels in the twentieth century. The language of the Greeks bespoke those ancient institutions as our American language does ours. There is similarity but also profound difference. Their language is inescapably linked to their experience and our language is inseparable from our very different experience. This is not just to say that the ancient Greeks *felt* differently about the objects of their experience than we do about the same objects. Their perceptions were different because their experience was different and therefore the *content* of their ideas and the words corresponding to them have no exact parallels for us.

Of course the experience is not totally different or communication would be impossible. There is a common ground of human existence and the fact of translation testifies to this basic human unity but the differences are considerable. One who has lived in a different culture gets the impression that the difficulty in conversing is bigger than the difference between the individuals involved. It is another people, another community with centuries old history, quite different than my own, which is addressing me in the person of this representative, and it is as a representative of my own people, molded by its institutions and attitudes that I must strive to understand.

That religion in particular rests on very private experience is often assumed in our modern western culture, but the supposition will not stand up to the facts. No doubt religion does deal with the deepest levels of human existence and touches each of us in the most private domains of our *psyche*, but those vague intuituions of another dimension to reality remain nameless without the influence of society. It is the influence of the community which gives them form and enables them to play an articulate part in our conscious thought and decisions. Without the images and language, the rituals and traditions, that come to us from the communities and societies to which we belong, this primitive and private experience would not be fully human. Without personal religious experience to anchor it, religious language is empty, but once formulated the religious language flows back upon the experience and shapes it. Nothing is more deeply personal than the grief of a mother whose child has just died, but when she kneels down and makes the sign of the cross and later is joined by her dear ones in a funeral liturgy that personal grief is gathered up into the story of Jesus' death and resurrection; the communal symbols and ritual give meaning to her personal tragedy. It is no longer isolated but is seen as part of the on-going story of that community which looks to Jesus to make sense of human existence. Without the personal pain the rituals would be hollow but the symbols and ritual do not simply give vent to the feeling; they humanize it, channel it in a particular direction, making it more than an animal cry of pain but rather an episode in an on-going community story, the key to which is found in the story of Jesus.

There is no way to draw a line between the private and the public or social in religion; they are too deeply intertwined. Practically speaking this means that treating religion—a morality too—as a purely private matter is an illusion. It means that letting each one "choose for himself" is an impossible goal. No one simply chooses for herself. Society is at work in every private decision. The question is what social group is acting and how mature and critical is the acceptance of that influence. Too often the church or religious community is conceived as the subsequent and secondary project of those who have first had their own private religious experience and then feel the need of sharing this experience with others. In fact the community has been present and active from the beginning even in the most private levels of that experience. Nor is this exclusively true in the areas of religious experience. Language, whether written, oral or ritual, is never simply the expression of what is already present in the *psyche*. Expressing our feelings or intuitions changes them, perhaps confirming and deepening them, perhaps modifying them, certainly integrating them into the wider community experience which has provided the language and symbols that serve as tools of expression.

What has been said above about the social character of all language is especially true of religious language. There is no creed or statement of belief, formal or informal, orthodox or heretical, traditional or ideosyncratic, which has meaning apart from the community which interprets it. Sounds and gestures do not carry meaning in themselves alone. They may point to objects or give rise to associations but the connection will be extremely vague especially since the object of religious discourse is not experienced directly. Similarly, rituals, whether inherited from past centuries or invented, now will be incomprehensible even to the one performing them apart from their social interpretation. Finally, the conclusions drawn from religion to guide moral conduct, however personal they may seem, are not reasoned out apart from the attitudes and understandings embedded in our language.

Could one say by way of vast generalization that nothing has become clearer to us in recent times than that everything is connected with everything else? The one thing we cannot do is to isolate anything from its surroundings, and this is a fatal blow to individualism. The insight itself would not be strange to the earliest Greek philosophers nor to the Biblical authors, but it is borne in on us from another direction by modern science. The great ambition of Descartes in the seventeenth century was to build a solid philosophy upon the foundation of clear and distinct ideas, each of which could stand on its own, independent of the rest. After a century of bitter religious controversy, this ambition is readily intelligible. How wonderful it would be if an individual could leave behind all the ambiguity of the past, all the obscurity arising from countless factors in human experience too shadowy to be drawn into full light, and build an unshakable edifice of certitude, independent of all the warring factions! But history has not been kind to Descartes's project. Clear and distinct ideas can only be bought at the price of unreality; reality does not come so neatly packaged. Only in mathematics and in formal logic—if even there—are ideas independent of the people who have them. In more concrete matters and certainly in questions of religion, morality and value, our ideas depend on many other factors in our personal experience. Our conclusions depend upon what segment of evidence we choose to concentrate on. How often do we discover in the course of an argument that what is at stake is not different conclusions drawn from the same evidence, but that different persons are lead in all sincerity by their different values and attitudes to concentrate on different parts of an almost unlimited field of evidence? They do not deny what others affirm but they weigh it differently because of the value system they bring to the argument. The futility of many theological debates, especially in the Reformation period, sprang from the illusion that one proposition was contending against another, whereas in fact the conflict was between different groups with different expectations. The proposition was relevant but not in isolation from the living persons who defend it. It is not surprising that few conversions resulted.

Paul Ricoeur has shown in a thorough analysis of various philosophical and religious explanations of the fact of evil how religious doctrines and philosophical positions rest upon more primitive symbols and only gradually well up from this opaque mass of human experience.[3] If we hasten prematurely to deal with the finished theological or philosophical expression which was only attained after centuries of reflection and controversy, and of more rudimentary attempts to give vocal or ritual expression to something only vaguely felt, we risk missing the depth and riches encapsulated in the final formulation. Once again the danger is to separate one facet of the truth from the matrix in which it is embedded.

Recently, too, we are coming to appreciate better the role imagination plays in all human learning. In a more rationalistic age the tendency was to consign imagination to the sphere of entertainment and relaxation at best and escapism at worst. Serious intellectuals at least in their working hours had no time for anything so frivolous, but psychologists think otherwise now. The line between what we perceive and what we imagine is thin and blurred. It is our imagination which directs our other faculties and determines in no small measure what meaning we will be able to find in the almost unlimited data of experience. Imagination is the open door to growth and discovery; when it is closed we are locked into our past.

Evolution and Interconnectedness

Perhaps the greatest obstacle to cutting reality into separate slices and treating the pieces as though they were self-contained and could be understood apart from their surroundings is the discovery of evolution. It has been remarked that evolution is not so much a particular theory as a dimension of all modern thought. We have learned in the physical sciences that sharp divisions between different classes of beings do not exist, one form shades off into another and it is difficult or impossible to define the boundaries. The division between biology, chemistry and physics, not to mention their numerous subdivisions, which seemed clear and definite enough not too long ago, has dissolved in obscurity. It is being widely recognized, for example, that the practice of medicine is as dependent upon psychology as upon anatomy. There is hardly a physical malady which is not intimately related to mental and emotional conditions. The kind of mechanistic viewpoint which could treat living organs like detachable parts of a machine has been thoroughly discredited. On the other hand, psychological states cannot be studied or dealt with apart from the organic conditions linked to them. Even language, which seemed the safe preserve of humanistic studies, is recognized by anthropologists like Claude Lévi-Strauss as an evolutionary development of some forms of animal behavior and consequently cannot be interpreted adequately without reference to its prehuman antecedents. Is there any scholar who has not felt the frustrating sense that it is never possible to cordon off any field for her own specialization? It is always necessary to make further excursions into related areas to understand with any adequacy her own particular and limited interest.

There was a time when evolution especially as it relates to human beings was seen as the great enemy of Christian belief. It appeared as the classic instance of conflict between "faith" and "science," because the data of biological research seemed to be in direct contradiction to the biblical record of creation. That time has passed at least for most Christian theologians. Instead we have here an example of how our understanding of revelation has been expanded, deepened and purified by contact with the scientific community. We have come to appreciate better than our forebears who were not in dialogue with modern science that God's action in creating our universe and his providence in guiding it do not belong to the tangible, material sphere that can be explored by natural science but to a totally different *order* of reality, and we have come to a more mature understanding of the sacred scriptures. If the conflict remains for some on both sides of the argument, that is due to a narrow, sectarian approach to the evidence, whether on the part of defenders of the Bible, who have closed their minds to scientific evidence and look to religion for the answer to scientific questions, or on the part of scientists who arbitrarily reject any form of knowledge which does not fit into the methodology of empirical science, and look to science for the answer to religious questions. Everyone recognizes how biased biblical fundamentalists can be, but religious people have no monopoly on prejudice.

As religious thinkers have moved beyond the rigid positions from which they confronted Darwinism and modern science in general during the nineteenth century (Teilhard de Chardin is only the most obvious example), leaders in science have left behind the confident materialism of that same age of scientific optimism. This is particularly true in the field of physics where the most exciting developments have taken place, but it applies in lesser degree to other fields. There is far less assurance that science has unraveled the workings of the universe will hold up as foundation stones in that project. In fact, that is to understate the degree to which modern physics, following the lead of Einstein, Heisenberg and many others, has demolished the paradigms of reality accepted as proven, scientific fact only a few generations ago. Where once scientists had expected that the laws and patterns discovered and codified in the heyday of Newtonian science would lead to a complete explanation of all the phenomena we experience and thus render superfluous any talk about a spiritual dimension of reality, the new physics has brought disillusionment. The startling discovery that subatomic particles do not conform at all to those laws and patterns has shaken the foundations of materialism and has lead to an unprecedented awareness on the part of leading contemporary scientists that even the world we can touch is infinitely more mysterious than we thought before and consequently an openness on their part to listen to other sources of enlightenment which would have been judged "unscientific" in simpler days. The breakdown of scientific certitudes has not assured a religious interpretation of the world but it has surely undercut the argument that science has proven religion false.[4]

It is true that even today many biologists persist in treating evolution as a full explanation of the origin of human life, replacing the doctrine of creation, but it is not scientific experimentation which forces this conclusion upon them but their own particular mind set, which excludes any source of truth other than the methodology appropriate to natural science. The most that scientific experimentation can tell us about the origin of humanity is the process by which it occurred; it can tell us literally nothing about its meaning and purpose. Science can perhaps tell us *HOW* the world originated; about the ultimate *WHY* it must remain silent. It has no instruments for even dealing with those questions of ultimate meaning, much less solving them. If a transcendent God is at work in every step of the process, and if this world and especially our human family is part of a story involving the Divine Persons, as Christians believe, there is no telescope or microscope that can capture the Divine action; it is reality of a different *kind* than can be dealt with in any laboratory. It can no more be refuted by scientific evidence than it can be proven by it. Agnostic scientists will insist, with a vehemence which suggests that more than academic factors are at stake, that questions of meaning and purpose must not even be asked, but there is no scientific reason for restricting human knowledge within the limits of empirical, scientific methodology. Human beings have always asked the larger questions and they are asking them more insistently today than at other times. The choice to exclude them from the arena of human reflection is an *a priori* choice made on some other basis than facts discovered in scientific experimentation. It is, in fact, an example of scientism rather than science and a violation of the cardinal principle we have been proposing in this book, in that one, partial approach to reality—namely the very fruitful approach of modern, empirical science—is given an exclusive and monopolistic place in human experience, a kind of scientific imperialism.

Mention of evolution evokes first of all the physical sciences and the development of higher forms of life from those which are more primitive, but the word can have a much wider sense and it is in that wider sense that we use it here. It can apply to cultural things as well, to ideas and patterns of living, thinking and praying. The discovery of evolution on the biological plane has been accompanied by its discovery on other planes as well. This has resulted in the conviction that nothing in our world—our intellectual, cultural and religious world included—comes full grown. It develops only gradually, rooted in the past but drawing upon all the environment that surrounds it. The consequence is that nothing can be separated abruptly from its surroundings and understood without reference to countless other factors which have influenced its growth. This has application to religious as well as secular concerns, to rituals and sacraments, dogmas and forms of religious organization. Superficially this might seem to deny the divine or supernatural character of the Christian religion, but only if we persist in thinking God must act according to the patterns of reality as they were known in centuries past. If evolution, in that wide sense of the term, the law of gradual and organic development, is really the pattern of our universe which modern science has discovered, it is hardly surprising that the transcendent God would act according to that pattern in bestowing his grace and revelation.

We began this section by observing that everything is connected with everything else and all we have been doing since is illustrating the great network of interaction in which human living and thinking takes place. To cut off one segment of our being from the rest is to condemn even the part we single out to sterility. Isolation means impoverishment. Only when all the streams which feed into our experience are flowing freely will health and growth be as full as possible. If this applies to different facets of our individual lives, it applies even more to human beings in community. Might this not serve as a definition of catholicity? A community is catholic when all the streams of wisdom and vitality are flowing into it and are channelled there into a great river.

As we indicated earlier the main enemy of such a dream is extreme individualism, the tendency to cut loose one fragment of the human inheritance and make it independent of the rest. The philosophical project of Descartes to make an absolutely new beginning and to build a system of knowledge accepting only clear and distinct ideas as building blocks for the new edifice and proceeding only when each step was secure beyond doubt, can serve as a model for this type of individualism. Descartes's plan collapsed relatively soon, but many other philosophers in succession took up the cause, bringing their own particular intellectual insights in place of Descartes', but sharing his fundamental ambition of developing one, self-contained, philosophical system that could be accepted and could serve as a touchstone for the whole of human knowledge. The series terminates in Hegel, who felt that his own great synthesis was the final step in philosophy. In a sense it was, in that after Hegel it seems widely recognized that the project itself is hopeless. No philosophy is big enough to capture the whole of reality. Human experience is too many faceted to submit to any one intellectual vision. The temptation to make one's own understanding absolute, to fit all reality into our own intellectual patterns is no doubt a perpetual temptation for mankind but it has never been more clearly a fantasy than at present.

Community Not Individual, the Center

Perhaps we have gotten lost in a maze of examples, which are at best only suggestions of a line of thought which deserves a more thorough development. It would be well to take our bearings. The burden of this chapter is that the unit of thought and action in things sacred as well as things secular must be the community, not the isolated individual. Centuries ago the "universal man" or woman, the polymath at home in all branches of knowledge, may have appeared as an almost attainable ideal. The expansion of knowledge in all directions since then has made even the most ambitious among us more humble. The greatest genius with the fullest education conceivable can command only a very partial view and its very partiality must produce some distortion. Wholeness can only pertain to the community and even then only to a community which is in principle as wide as humanity.

Put in these terms the application to our topic is evident. No individual can be catholic; only a community; the individual can be catholic only in so far as he or she is part of the community and is bathed in the wholeness of that community. If Jesus Christ wishes his church to be catholic, that church must be a true community not a collection of individuals each of whom has experienced a personal conversion. Community must enter into the inner fabric of Christian life. Of course, belonging to a community is no guarantee of catholicity. Sectarian communities can be more narrow than individual persons; their effect can be to reinforce what is most provincial in their members.

Developments in every field of human learning within recent centuries have brought to light the profoundly social character of all human life and activity, as we have tried to show. Humanity is not fully present in any individual human being. Of its very nature human existence reaches out beyond the individual not just, as with the animals and things around us, that we need much else to survive, but because the spiritual world we touch in those activities which are most properly human is, in a mysterious but real sense, the common property of mankind, incapable of being fenced off into separate plots. Humans are not first separate beings who then join societies, as many seventeenth century thinkers like Hobbes and Locke believed, but social from the start. We might even say social before they are individual in the sense that human consciousness can only grow within community. Without community human existence is impossible. Poets and philosophers have taught us such things in their own way in the distant past but modern science in all its branches has filled in the details.

Love Is Communal

In our own investigation we have concentrated on the intellectual side of man's social nature, but the same case could be made more easily for the affective and volitional sides. One of the achievements of modern psychology has been to vindicate from a secular perspective the importance and centrality of love in human existence. S. Blanton put the alternative bluntly in the title of his well known book—*Love or Perish.*[5] The unprecedented desire for intimacy in our civilization, the popularity of communes where new forms of family groupings are encouraged with a view to more and better human sharing among its members, and the repudiation of any structures, however efficient and promising technologically, which do violence to the human need for companionship: all of these developments and many more testify that the dilemma Blanton proposes is widely felt in our society. No doubt fads are involved in some cases and they will disappear with time but the underlying need is deep in human nature as its resurgence against the depersonalizing trends of our times indicates.

Modern research has been led by its own evidence to discover what was present from the start in Christianity. Jesus made love the supreme commandment, the pivot on which swings the whole of Christian morality, but it is possible to ask a further question. Was this an arbitrary choice? Could he as easily have selected a different virtue? Is love the all important obligation because Jesus said it was or did Jesus teach the pre-eminence of love because "he knew what was in man,"[6] because women and men are so made by God that they can only be fulfilled in love? Surely the latter is the case. Human beings are incomplete in themselves. We are so structured that it is only by reaching out to others and renouncing self sufficiency that we can hope to be happy. To pick up Jesus' own metaphor, the grain of wheat must fall into the ground and die in order to be fruitful,[7] not because God has commanded it but because it is the nature of a blade of wheat to realize its potential in no other way. The clinging to its own life and independence is "to remain alone," to wither away in sterility. Similarly, for ourselves to hold tenaciously to our own individual resources whether of soul or body and to close ourselves off from others must result in stunted growth, not because God will punish us for our pride but because the resources for growth are in our brothers and sisters. If we refuse these resources it is our own self-sufficiency which condemns us to stagnation. The Christian commandment of love rests upon an anthropological foundation. Healthy human life is inescapably life in community and this applies in religion as much as elsewhere.

This may put at rest the fears many people feel in the face of the overwhelmingly social character of being human, demonstrated by contemporary psychology. It is one of the tragedies of recent centuries that community appears to many as the enemy of the individual, as though we could only attain personal identity at the expense of community and likewise what is gained for the community must be wrested from the individual. Exactly the opposite is the case! We can only achieve individual identity and maturity within community. It is only in our relationship with others that we become full persons; alone our humanity and our personal growth are aborted. Paradoxically what Christian faith affirms about Father, Son and Holy Spirit in the inner life of God is reflected in human experience. the more persons are united to each other on the personal level, the greater is their difference as persons. True unity does not destroy but enhances individuality and distinctness. A happy marriage is the best example; the partners are free to develop their own personality inn a way otherwise impossible because they know they are accepted in all their individuality in love. Of course there is always a treat in human societies that community will be pursued in a sub-human manner on a biological or even a mechanical plane without respect for the personal freedom that constitutes the highest level of human existence and it is important to be constantly on guard against this danger, but if, on the other hand, community is rejected in the name of personal freedom, the freedom which remains will be thin indeed.

Anthropological Implications of Jesus' Commandment To Love

We have been discussing love and community on that level where the Gospel makes contact with humanistic psychology. The Christian message goes much further. The love which Jesus made the distinguishing mark of his followers is more than the human need to reach out to others which psychologists have recognized. It is no less than "the love of God poured out in our hearts through the Holy Spirit who has been given to us,"[8] and its roots are not ultimately in human nature but in the eternal life of Father, Son and Holy Spirit into which Christ, our Lord has introduced us. The community which provides the social ingredient for the religious life of Christians is more than human fellowship. It is nothing less than the body of Christ, so often referred to by St. Paul, animated by the Holy Spirit and held together by stronger ties than any psychological methods can uncover. To explore in detail these supernatural aspects of community is to open up great riches of Christian spirituality, but it is outside our scope at present. What I want to emphasize here is the implications of these New Testament truths upon our image of humankind and in particular the image of humankind as social. They tell us that the individual man or woman cannot stand alone, cannot even be conceived alone. Can you imagine human existence if God had created only one human being? Whatever such a monstrous creature might be, its existence would not be human in any recognizable sense of the word. When it is said that man cannot stand alone, the religiously minded person may instinctively think of the need for God and surely it is the most fundamental need of all but it is not the only one. We need other human beings, too, and we need them on every level of our being. In spirituality and religion as elsewhere community reaches to the inner core of human existence.

To assert with St. Paul that the whole law is summed up in love[9] is to deliver a death blow to individualism. The center of gravity for Christian conduct is in others, not in ourselves and rugged individualism is as contrary to this ideal in matters of worship and religious faith as it is in economics. Significantly there is here a distinguishing feature of Christianity. All religion calls for self-transcendence; it demands that we surrender our fixation on ourselves and reach out beyond our selfish concerns, but the transcendence to which we are summoned is sometimes conceived as vague and formless. Christians recognize that the final goal of all our striving is the mysterious reality of God himself, infinitely beyond our understanding and our language, however they believe that this infinite God can be found in my neighbor. Transcendence takes shape in the very definite and often disconcerting form of my neighbor. The journey away from self-centeredness does not lead directly and exclusively to God but through my fellow men and women. The vertical thrust of religion upward to God himself gathers up and blends with the horizontal thrust outward to other human beings. Likewise the life line through which I receive from God his grace and revelation passes through my brothers and sisters without compromising the directness of our relation with God, since the fact that God uses mediators to communicate with us does not cancel out his immediate contact with all creatures.

Perhaps we have not appreciated the revolutionary implications of the description Jesus gives of the final judgement. He makes salvation depend not upon asceticism or contemplation but upon our conduct toward other human beings. To those who are saved the judge will say, "I was hungry and you gave me food, ...thirsty and gave me drink, ...as often as you did it for one of my least brothers, you did it for me."[10] Most often this passage is used to motivate Christians to the practice of charity but its interest here is the light it casts on the social nature of humanity. It is more than an exhortation to brotherly love; it is implicitly a statement about the connection between man's relation to his fellows and man's relation to God. The same Jesus who said, "Whoever has seen me has seen the Father"[11] identifies himself with other human beings who come into our lives. Our relationship with other women and men is integrated into our relationship to God. This is not to minimize the value of solitary prayer and ascetical practice, as the rest of the New Testament and the Christian tradition demonstrate abundantly, nor is it to imply that eastern religions neglect the obligation of religious people toward their fellow human beings, but it does seem clear that the vertical relation of the human family to God and the horizontal relation of people toward other flesh and blood human beings in all the concreteness of their life on earth, are joined together in a unique fashion by Christian faith. If one accepts the Christian revelation, mankind is more social than we could have suspected without it.

****

To sum up, the only Christianity which is commensurate with the needs of our times is one which is catholic, because we have learned better than any of our ancestors that human living does not occur in isolated cases but only as situated within a wider network of interaction of people upon each other and of humanity with the rest of the universe. Indeed we must stretch the meaning of community to include in some way not only the men and women who are its members but also the world they touch and are touched by, as we suggested in discussing the wider meaning of catholicity in the last chapter. The only claim to truth which can stand up against a scepticism fortified by so much new evidence that every system of philosophy, theology or science is partial, time-conditioned and destined to be superseded, is a claim to truth made for a living community rather than for an individual. Individuals and small closed sects can hold on to their separate visions with unshakable confidence; their mutual support will confirm them in their vision and help them to suppress doubts; but others outside the group will recognize the relativity and the distortion of that vision. Consequently the others could not accept such a vision without intellectual dishonesty. Modern communications and the findings of philosophy and the sciences have broken down the barriers which protected closed societies in the past. The temptation to relativism and scepticism has never been stronger than in our times, and yet the Christian message is as much addressed to the twentieth century as to any other. If it is to be delivered effectively, the communitarian dimensions of that message must be developed to the full and lived out in a community which is, in the richest sense, catholic.

Notes

1. This is not to suggest that the epistemology of the great medieval philosophers was so simplistic, but it is probably accurate enough for the ordinary person and even in the case of the great medieval philosophers they lacked the scientific data on perception and knowledge which demonstrate so forcefully subjective factors.

2. Erich Fromm, *Escape From Freedom* (N.Y.: Farrar & Rinehart, 1941).

3. Paul Ricoeur, *The Symbolism Of Evil,* trans. Emerson Buchanan (N.Y.: Harper & Row, 1967).

4. A detailed development of the scientific side of what I have been saying here, supported by numerous quotations from contemporary scientists, will be found in Arthur Koestler, *Janus: A Summing Up* (London: Hutchinson & Co.,1978) especially Chapters 9 and 13.

See also John F. Haught, *The Cosmic Adventure: Science, Religion And The Quest For Purpose* (N.Y.: Paulist, 1981).

In the final segment of an outstanding series of films on world religions entitled "The Long Search" and produced for PBS, several distinguished scientists testified to the new scientific openness to religious data.

5. S. Blanton with E. Robinson, *Love Or Perish* (N.Y.: Simon & Schuster, 1959).

6. Jn. 2:25.

7. Jn. 12:24.

8. Rom. 5:5.

9. Rom. 13:9.

10. See Mt. 25:31-46.

11. Jn. 14:9.

Chapter Three

A Community of Dialogue

In the previous chapter we argued that only a community can be catholic; catholicity necessarily escapes the individual. Let us take a further step in this chapter. Only a community which of its very nature is open to all can honestly be called catholic. This is obvious enough if the word is taken at its face value, but its implications call for further reflection. As long as there is anything about a community which necessarily limits its appeal to a particular group; as long as there is in the essential make-up of that community anything which repels or alienates any class, race, nation or temperament, the community is not fully catholic.

One might conclude from this that catholicity is an impossible ideal. Whatever exists is particular; it is marked by the characteristics peculiar to its own time and place. Every community bears the imprint of the people who make it up, their culture, their customs, their limited knowledge and vision. Inevitably then what renders the community congenial to some, will for that very reason alienate others. The more it adapts itself to one culture, the less inviting it becomes to others. The conclusion is justified. No empirical community, no community, that is, as it exists and can be experienced at a particular historical moment can be fully catholic. Catholicity in the full range of its meaning, like any other essential attribute of the church of Christ, is applicable to the church only if one sees in her more than any empirical test can uncover. To say that the church is catholic is a judgement of faith not an observation of experience. It is only because the believer discerns beneath the external, observable reality of particular women and men, marked by all the particularities of their culture, an invisible Power of infinite potentialities that she can seriously claim that this particular community is catholic. It is not and cannot be catholic in so far as it is observable. It is only when all the dimensions of its reality are taken into consideration that the claim makes sense. The church is catholic because she is the "body of Christ." The church is catholic because the proximate agencies by which she acts externally are energized by the Holy Spirit of God.

But it is not enough to appeal to the ultimate Source of the church's life to understand the meaning of catholicity. Let us not imagine that the union of God with his covenanted people at any particular time in history makes that people catholic in itself. There is an intermediate step. Catholicity is not a direct gift of God to any definite group of people. It is a gift that belongs to the people as a whole and is mediated partially and imperfectly to particular segments of the people, in so far as that present segment of believers, limited as it is in time and space, is in communion with all the rest of God's people at all other times and in all other places. Catholicity describes the whole of God's dealings with his people from the beginning of creation to the final triumph of Christ's second coming. Only in the complete panorama of all history is the integrated pattern of God's plan revealed. Bracket any part of it, cut off any segment from interaction with the rest and the whole design will not appear. Catholicity is more than communion between God and man; it is also communion of men and women with each other in God, communion of all creation centered in and deriving from God.

In stressing the mysterious and invisible aspect of catholicity as a truth of faith, we must, nonetheless, beware of the temptation to separate visible from invisible, divine from human in the church. The mature countenance of the bride of Christ will not be seen until the *parousia*, but it will not be the face of a total stranger. Each phase of development prepares for the next and is congruous with it. The features may be blemished and scarred; there may be regression as well as positive growth, but like a sequence of photographs that record a person's history from infancy to old age, the same personality will be discernable throughout. At the present stage of salvation history catholicity like holiness is a question of degree. It is more a task than an accomplishment, more a commission to be fulfilled than a gift already received. What is essential is the thrust toward that final form. To be catholic at the present stage of salvation history means above all to be open, to resist everything which isolates, paralyzes or confines. Open to present, past and future. It is as much a fault to be indifferent to the past as to be fixated on it.

If catholicity is properly a quality of the whole community, taking that expression in its widest extension, in which here and now segments of the community may participate but which they never definitively embody, then the catholicity of any particular segment, whether local church or universal church at any particular time, is its congruity with other segments. The congruity in question is not geometrical; it does not demand an identical form nor the same dimensions but only that the parts fit together, that they can rest upon each other, one correcting the imbalance of the other. It calls for family resemblance not carbon copies. What it does rule out is discreteness, blockage, isolation. For instance, a catholic future is not prepared for by an individualistic present. An exclusively spiritual religion is not congruous with a faith that tries to leaven the whole world, nor is a Christianity reduced to pure humanism consistent with a tradition of prayer and spirituality. When the seeds of one epoch are uprooted rather than cultivated in another, congruity is lacking. Development need not be unilinear; patterns of growth differ and what was prominent at one period or in one place may be dormant in the next; one age will emphasize and even overemphasize one aspect of the total Christian tradition and the succeeding age will react against the excess. Opposition is a form of continuity as well as agreement, but when one group of Christians shuts itself up within its own viewpoints and practices and blocks out everything else, that group has become a sect and not an expression of catholic Christianity.

The Dialectical Process

In summary, a community can be catholic only if it is a community of dialogue. Let us explore the many faces of dialogue. It was Hegel more than anyone else who showed us that the model for progress in learning is not the solitary scholar locked in his own study and drawing further conclusions from the same evidence and the same principles, but the debate between adversaries, one denying what the other affirms, each challenging the other and by their confrontation leading to new insights richer than either could produce alone. Truths like persons cannot flourish in isolation. Also like persons, truths can wither without exercise. In a genuine sense they are no less true than previously but their vitality can be drained and their power to move hearts can be lost. How painfully we see this in the case of Christian dogma! The confrontation between Christian dogma and opposing viewpoints can be painful and even dangerous but without it doctrine is sterile. A church which is catholic will be one where tradition is not in secure possession, unruffled by contact with new and apparently hostile trends, but a place where controversy can be carried on, in a spirit of charity and deep loyalty to Christ, to be sure, but vigorously.

Communities: Open or Closed?

In this connection it needs to be said that the stress on community so characteristic of our own times is not necessarily congenial to catholicity. What people are often seeking in community today is a refuge from dissension. They want comforting companionship, an escape from the competition, tension and confusion that produce so many ulcers and nervous breakdowns. The desire is legitimate and the community of believers should respond to it—but not to it alone.

In the language of contemporary sociology there are two kinds of social groupings, the German terms for which have become classic: *gesellschaft*, which may be roughly translated as a contractual society, and *gemeinschaft*, which we might call a "taken-for-granted" society. The former is deliberately chosen, its members belong because they share consciously the same objectives as their fellows; often it is characterized by warm human friendship. The latter, on the other hand, is generally a larger unit; it tends to be taken for granted rather than consciously chosen; typically one is born into it, for example, a nation or a world wide church, rather than becoming a member because of personal conviction.

There are, of course, no clear boundaries between the two kinds of social unit; they overlap each other, but in outline there is difference enough to make the distinction useful. It is the small, intimate community which is attractive today and the larger, taken-for-granted association is spurned as unworthy of the name of community. And nowhere is this more the case than in religion. What many people are seeking in their worship and spirituality is genuine fellowship. In a fragmented society where so many institutions that once brought us together, like the family and humanized environments for work, have broken down, believers understandably look to their church for the experience of companionship with each other as well as with God. And rightly so, it is of the very nature of Christianity to draw us together in love. Still an exclusive emphasis on the contractual type of community will not produce a community of dialogue but one whose members confirm rather than challenge each other. Outsiders, the troublesome or just the different will be subtly excluded. The congregation will close in upon itself.

In past centuries Roman Catholics have characteristically looked upon the church as a *gemeinschaft* type of social group. The experience of fellowship has seemed less important to them that it did to Protestant Christians and it was natural to see the church as a very wide reality, one that pre-existed its present members by many centuries and was there for all to join. The local parish or congregation was secondary as were the social ties that bound parishioners to each other and to their pastors. More recently in this as in many other ways, Catholics have been appropriating typically "Protestant" values, while Protestants have become increasingly sensitive to the wider, more ecumenical dimensions of the church. Efforts have been made on the Catholic side to bring the worshippers together, literally and figuratively, around the altar of the Lord, to heighten the *feeling* as well as the spiritual reality of oneness. Monika Hellwig points out in a perceptive chapter which has inspired what is said here,[1] that necessary as this new emphasis on felt community is, it would be unfortunate if it edged out the traditional Roman Catholic concern for the larger community, larger, that is, than the people with whom we associate consciously in our Christian living, large enough to include people we have never known. The communion at which Christian faith is aiming is after all more than felt community. It is unity in the Holy Spirit, and the warm human fellowship which should bind together the local congregation is only the local expression of a unifying force as wide as the world. It should certainly be wide enough to keep the local congregation from folding in upon itself and make it receptive to the challenges and differences which make for growth.

The most evident strength of the Roman Catholic tradition may be its success in keeping very diverse and even opposed groups together within the church. The human reason for this success, I suggest, is the acceptance of a world wide structure of government, whose authority is seen as coming from God. Ultimately unity within the church is the work of the Holy Spirit, but history has shown repeatedly that if this divine, invisible unity is not mediated by external governmental structures, factionalism will pull the community apart. When conditions are harmonious, unity appears as a great value, but when divisions arise, whether in doctrine or in policy or even in cultural style, opposing groups will soon convince themselves that they are the only ones responding to the Spirit's guidance and that loyalty to God demands separation from the rest. Where a centralized authority exists and especially where that authority is recognized as more than a human agency of the society to defend its own interests, but as itself the voice of God, there is a better chance that differences will not end in division. The function of the centralized authority, if it is exercised wisely, will not be to reduce differences to sameness but to keep them in healthy tension within the wider community. It is not difficult for a small contractual society to hold together. It does so to some extent by differentiating itself from others, coming closer together the narrower it becomes. Its unity is proportionate to its exclusiveness. The greater challenge for a church which claims a mission to the whole human family is to keep the unity of its present members from becoming a barrier against the world outside.

The one church of Jesus Christ is made up of many small churches and Roman Catholic theology is giving more attention than ever before to the local church, recognizing its integrity as an incarnation of Christ in its particular place in its own right and not after the fashion of a branch office of the church universal, but these local churches and their members must be part of a wider communion in order to be catholic. And *communion*, not just community, is what the church is all about. The latter word implies external relationship, while the former goes much deeper; it suggests the supernatural bonds which tie this community together. There is more in common to the community of believers than what they themselves are conscious of. Their human fellowship, their collaboration in common goals, the comfort and support they supply each other are rooted in a mysterious unity with the risen Jesus and with his Spirit. Communion by a happy association links the social unity of Christians with the Eucharist, which is its center and its source. They are not one with each other only because they think and feel alike but because they are fed by the same food. Their *koinonia* (communion) with each other, St. Paul tells them, is the product of their *koinonia* in the body and blood of Christ.

Is not the cup of blessing we bless a sharing in the blood of Christ? And is not the bread we break a sharing in the body of Christ? Because the loaf of bread is one, we, many though we are, are one body, for we all partake of the one loaf.[2]

It can only be suggested here, without digressing from the limited point we are making in this chapter, but the word *communion* has a rich history in Christian tradition especially among eastern Christians.[3] Seeing the church as a communion rather than just a community would correct the tendency too common among western Christians today to define the church in terms of her externals and to identify oneness with an *experience* of oneness. Externals like laws, offices and officers belong within the community of Christians; human collaboration with Christ in building the Kingdom cannot occur without them. They are integral to the process, not accessories, but they are only the surface of a largely subterranean force, drawing the whole human family into one great project. Likewise the unity we possess in Jesus Christ is much greater than the unity we experience. Whether they know it or not, all are somehow really one in Jesus Christ, if we can say with St. Paul, "just as a single offense brought condemnation to all, a single righteous act brought all acquittal and life."[4]

In summary, what we have been pleading for in these last few pages is that the present enthusiasm for felt community, for the formation of intimate groups of believers sharing life together on many levels and for deepening and personalizing the ties between parishioners in all too often impersonal parishes, should not drowned out the call to a community as wide as the world. If it did, the unmistakable desire for community in out times would turn into an enemy of catholicity. To be catholic a community must be the home of dialogue, which is a place where tensions are sometimes exacerbated rather than resolved, and walls are not high enough to provide security and comfort for those inside. Let us proceed to examine in some detail how dialogue works.

Truths in Tension

Pascal observed that the source of all heresies is the failure to comprehend the harmony of two opposing truths. Christian history provides abundant confirmation for this judgement. Pelagians stress human freedom but forget God's grace; Jansenists cling to grace but are willing to sacrifice freedom; sometimes it is the divinity of Christ that gets exclusive emphasis and sometimes his humanity; the social aspects of Christian life are emphasized to the detriment of personal conversion, or personal conversion is so valued that everything social is forgotten; the eschatological dimension is so prominent that the Gospel call to work for justice on earth goes unheard, or Christians are so intent on building a better world that they deny or ignore eternal life. In every case the failure is not total falsehood but one-sidedness. The problem is that our minds, and our hearts too, can only fasten on one thing at a time. What we fasten on is usually true and important but outside our minds it mingles with other truths that complicate it. No one statement and no one system does justice to the truth. It is necessary to keep making statements, many of them seemingly contradictory, to be faithful to the demands of truth. The final statement will never be made, because God and his creation will always exceed our minds and our language.

That great forerunner of ecumenism, Nicholas of Cusa, appealed to the "*coincidentia oppositorum*," the coincidence of opposites. That is the secret of dialectics and both words are important. It is opposing or apparently contradictory propositions which are brought together, but they are not laid on top of each other, but made to coincide, to interpenetrate each other, the one breaking open the understanding of the other and expanding it. What is at stake is argument, controversy, rather than bland conversation, but argument where neither contestant will end up in the same place where they began.

An example may bring the abstract principle down to earth. Christian faith and indeed all religion and morality suppose the reality of human freedom—we are what we are and do what we do (within limits) by choice and not by necessity and we are consequently responsible for our actions. But there are seemingly opposite truths. Christians are just as firmly committed to the belief that God is absolute master of all his creatures, not excluding those who possess free will. Furthermore, Christians also believe with St. Paul, that we are not free to do anything which will please God and enable us to achieve our destiny by ourselves alone. For this we are totally dependent upon God's action within us, which we have no power to command. Add to this the abundant evidence from secular science that human beings are conditioned by their heredity and environment, all of which appears at first glance to negate self-determination or freedom. We are dealing then with conflictual assertions.

One way of dealing with the conflict is to come down hard on one side, the one we find most persuasive and close our ears and our minds to evidence pointing in another direction. Another solution is to live with the conflict, refusing to abandon genuine evidence on either side, even while acknowledging that we cannot harmonize one with the other. This latter solution is reasonable enough. By what logic can we claim the ability to answer every question which presents itself? Perhaps a satisfactory resolution calls for more evidence than is available to us. All of us must live with many unanswered questions. But here dialogue can help. What may emerge from the argument, short of a definitive answer, is a more complex notion of freedom and a more mature understanding of God and of his dealings with creatures. Faith will not be lost but neither will it remain static.

Dialectical method is not a discovery of Hegel or of recent times. Back in the thirteenth century Thomas Aquinas followed dialectical method in his classic *Summa Theologica*. Thomas begins each topic by proposing objections to the position he is going to defend and after he has explained that position, he concludes the section by responding to the objections with which he began. From the Middle Ages to very recent times among Scholastic philosophers and theologians the privileged academic exercise was the disputation, where one student's task was to propose and defend a position in dialogue with those whose job was to attack it. But today we appreciate better than the medievals the dynamic and developmental quality of all truth. Whereas Thomas and his contemporaries used dialectical method to refute adversaries and to defend the truth, which they conceived in a relatively static fashion, today we acknowledge a more positive and constructive service which dialectics can provide. For us dialectics is more than a pedagogical method of deducing further consequences from truths already vaguely known. It is a necessary way of moving forward the process of knowing and mastering a changing world.

From a philosophical point of view, it would be well to notice the connection between dialectical method and analogy. Traditionally there are three ways of using words and concepts: univocal, equivocal and analogous. A univocal idea remains the same in all its uses. When, for example, we speak of an oak tree and an elm tree, the word "tree" retains the same meaning in both uses. Elms do differ from oaks but our minds are able to focus on something they have in common; what differentiates them from each other is external to their "treeness." There is a certain rigidity to a univocal concept but a rigidity with very positive results. It makes possible scientific discourse, because in mathematical and physical science we can be confident that the word or symbol will have the same meaning everywhere, thereby providing a solid and verifiable foundation for experimentation and conclusions. Equivocation, on the contrary, is a kind of word game. The same word or name is used of more than one object but the only thing the objects have in common is the name itself. "Match" can refer to a piece of wood used to light a candle or to an athletic contest. Less innocently an advertiser or a demagogue may try to profit from the associations evoked by a name, even when the association has no basis in fact. Equivocation is language out of contact with objective reality. It is the path of illusion or deception or at best escape.

Analogy falls between the two. Unlike equivocation it is grounded in objective reality not just in language and thought, but it is less rigid than univocal thinking. It is open to association, to aspects of reality which cannot be pinned down; it is aware of the ambiguity and obscurity of our understanding of the world and sensitive to symbolisms that cannot be specified with accuracy. Analogy is testimony to the limitations of our knowledge and our language, to the fact that the reality we can fit neatly into our categories is only a fragment of wider reality, which impinges on our consciousness only indirectly. For one who thinks univocally, autumn is a climatological phenomenon, measurable in terms of temperature, wind velocity, etc.; analogy, without denying any of this "hard" data, finds in autumn a suggestion of mortality, of the finite character of all things. For the poet, as a person singularly attuned to analogy, autumn raises questions about ultimate meaning and purpose, and who is to say that these suggestions are any less objective than computerized data, simply because they point to reality beyond the range of the computer? They are reality of a different *kind*, to be sure, than information which can be quantified, but this does not make them unreal or purely imaginary. Without some appreciation of and sympathy for analogy, religious thought and language is impossible. Indeed, it may be that the greatest obstacle to religion on the part of pragmatically minded persons is their identification of univocal knowledge with knowledge pure and simple and their refusal, more often unreflecting than deliberate, to accept analogy as a genuine source of knowledge.

We have been speaking of concepts and reasoning but the same could be said in some measure of images. Images are more fluid than concepts but it makes sense none the less to speak of univocal as opposed to analogous imagination. In science and pragmatic concerns univocal imagination has great advantages but how much dryness and stagnation can be traced to rigid and static images! Our images and consequently our expectations can be *too* clear and consistent. We can be more effectively imprisoned by the limits of our imagination than by any external restraints. So often nothing is more healing than an enlargement of our images.[5]

It is not surprising that in selecting a title for his masterful study of the methodology peculiar to Catholic theology, David Tracy chose to call his book *The Analogical Imagination*.[6] Analogy is the correlate of catholicity. It is the refusal of individualism. It will not accept the limits of any human mind or of all human minds together as the boundaries of reality. Analogy requires us to keep our minds and hearts and imaginations endlessly open and receptive to data and suggestions, however faint and obscure, coming from all directions.

As a means of bringing the rather theoretical points we have been making to a more practical and psychological level, I should like to borrow an expression from William F. Lynch, S.J. in a little book in which he develops and exemplifies in a far more scholarly way the thesis proposed in this chapter.[7] Lynch speaks about the "integrating mind." Faced with contraries we can respond with an either-or mentality. It is the easiest and most emotionally satisfying way to respond; it delivers us from ambiguity and gives us a sense of self-righteousness; it dispenses us from listening to our adversaries because we are convinced they are simply wrong and evil, thus we need not come to grips with their arguments. But as Pascal says, it is the root of all heresies; it is divisive, pulling people apart into hostile camps and digging deeper trenches between them. Lynch sees it as a threat to national survival and even to the survival of the kind of free, democratic society we have developed in the west, because it undermines the minimal conditions for dialogue necessary for such a society to exist.

There is another way of dealing with contraries. Let us call it with Lynch, the "integrating mind." It brings them together rather than keeping them apart. Its motto is both-and, rather than either-or. It recognizes that almost anything any sincere person says seriously is at least partly true and it is more interested in accepting and assimilating that kernel of truth than in striking down the error which may be mixed with it. In religious matters its goal is to convert rather than to conquer. It is secure in the truth it possesses and is determined to make its own contribution to the human conversation but it does not see that contribution as supplanting and obliterating other contributions but as completing them and in turn being completed by them. We could as easily call it the "catholic mind" or better the "catholic spirit," because what is at stake is more than a method of reasoning but a spiritual disposition, an attitude or point of view based on a peculiarly catholic way of looking at the world and nourished by centuries of tradition, especially within the Roman Catholic communion. It assumes that in spite of all the evil around us the fundamental drive in all people is for truth and good and it is premised on the belief that all history everywhere is part of one and the same divine plan, centered in Jesus Christ.

Yet we should not wax lyrical about this integrating mind; it has its dangers as well as its many benefits and those dangers have called forth protest in all ages and in particular "Protestantism" in modern times. Essentially the danger is that of watering down the truth which has been given to us personally in the name of some wider truth given to all humanity, or at least blunting its force. Its extreme form is a kind of amorphous tolerance, devoid of any conviction, much less of enthusiasm for a cause. Any statement can be accepted because none is genuinely believed. Of course, this is a caricature of the integrating mind we are advocating here. The antidote is to recognize that for the individual the choice is often either-or rather than both-and. Many times we must choose between alternatives, even when our understanding of them is quite imperfect and we must stand behind our choice resolutely, accepting the consequences if we are mistaken. We must resign ourselves as individuals to being somewhat unbalanced. Wholeness and perfect balance belong to the community not to the individual and only to the community in its very widest dimensions, as we argued in the opening section of this chapter. The individual Christian must follow the light as she sees it, forcefully, courageously and with conviction. The common search for truth will be hampered if she does not. Still a little humility will do no harm. Each of us can appreciate that our own vision is always partial, not that we are thereby dispensed from following it with all the energy we can summon up, but that we are prevented from identifying our own vision with absolute truth. Only God sees the whole picture, and if the truth which seems so evident to us is not accepted or it appears to be contradicted by new evidence, we will not be shattered but will find peace and the patience to keep searching, confident that whatever truth we have discovered or good we have done, will find its place in that whole picture, perhaps not exactly as we imagined it but fully there.

I want to return briefly to the observation that the dangers of the integrating mind have called forth protest throughout Christian history. This is itself an instance of dialectical tension. The prophet or protestor speaks for the either-or rather than the both-and. His providential role is to call attention to a truth or value which has been allowed to merge into an undifferentiated and largely forgotten background but which, because of the circumstances of the time needs to be brought to center stage. Too balanced and nuanced a view would dim the fire of conviction and enthusiasm needed to fulfill his mission. Without prophets and protest the salt of christian life would lose it savor, but with nothing but prophets the church would become fanatical. The truth or value the prophet is proclaiming tends to become dislodged from the total matrix of Christian experience and thereby distorted. We cannot blame the prophet for this; the risk is intrinsic to his vocation, but if prophecy ends in schism, where the balancing factors of the whole tradition cannot smooth its rough edges and prevent exaggeration, the prophet is betraying later generations of his followers. Different times require different emphases and the day will come when an emphasis different from that of the originating prophet will be needed. Without communion with other Christians and with the whole tradition, that new emphasis will not be available.

It is time to pull together the strands of our argument. The dialectical process refutes individualism and thus it reinforces my contention that the search for truth is necessarily a communal project. Any wholeness of vision achieved by any individual, however brilliant, is a premature wholeness, because no individual sees more than a part of reality and given the interconnectedness of things, even that part is seen awry to some extent because of the angle of vision. In the synthesis reached by an individual, opposites are reconciled in a way which does not do them full justice. The "integrating mind" we have been praising is the mind of a community; the individual can share in it only by sharing in a community wide enough to draw the opposites together without dissolving in the least their distinctness. According to faith there is only one community capable of doing this: the church of Jesus Christ.

Dialogue Expanded

Dialogue and dialectics are intellectual terms. In using them we run the risk of placing excessive emphasis on the intellectual side of Christian life, therefore the word *dialogue*, as we have used it in the title of this chapter, has to be expanded beyond its dictionary meaning to do justice to the point we are making. Dialectics is an academic and intellectual branch of the larger reality we have been calling dialogue and here we wish to expand that larger category even further. The church of Jesus Christ is more than a community of ideas; it is a communion of life, and essential as doctrine is for Christians, life is more than thinking.

Dialogue is a form of interaction between partners or contestants where the end product is better than either partner could have produced alone. Earlier in this chapter the partners in question were mainly different doctrines, viewpoints and ideas, but in the family of believers sharing life in Jesus, could not the interaction be, just as significantly, between different temperaments, different generations, different tastes and different styles of living?

It is a commonplace observation but not less important for being such that diversity enriches a group. Pluralism, political and cultural, is so widely valued at present that no defense of it is necessary here. Not too long ago the ideal set before Americans was that of the "melting pot," where many different people could be fused into a new, homogeneous nation, but we now recognize that to dissolve their cultural differences is to impoverish people and the kind of monolithic unity it may bring is bought at too high a price. Movements among black people to assert and cultivate their own identity proudly and similar movements among other ethnic groups have exposed the flaw in the melting pot model, but we have to go no further than the letters of St. Paul to learn the same lesson. Paul insists more than once that diversity in structure and function of its members, far from being an enemy to the unity and health of the body—physical or social—is a positive benefit.[8] It is true that in the passages cited, Paul is directly concerned with a diversity of spiritual gifts and offices within the unity of one church community, but the principle he invokes, if it is correct, must apply to the wider cultural differences at issue here.

What does this cultural interweaving look like? Different races, nations, and classes impress their own distinctive features upon their rituals, customs, and laws, their language, art and music, even their way of relating to each other. The differences are usually subtle and difficult to describe precisely, but life in a Scottish village has a different feel than life in the middle of Chicago; family, work and education are experienced differently in Japan than in Portugal; the sensitivities of a primitive people are worlds apart from those of a modern urban dweller. Each has strengths that can complement the other where it is weak.

Let me illustrate what I am driving at. A priest friend of mine, whose background had been almost exclusively the American academic world, spent a considerable period living with the people in a rural village in Mexico. He spoke of the irritation and frustration he experienced at first at the delays and inefficiency of practical services. When the plumbing broke down one Saturday, for instance, they were informed that the plumber did not work on the weekend but would be around on Monday. Then he gradually came to appreciate the different values and priorities of that culture. Is efficiency more important than friendship, than family life, than the leisurely pattern of living necessary to enjoy the simple pleasures of life? My friend was changed and enriched by that contact with a world quite different than his own and no doubt his hosts profited not only from his own generous spirit but also from the practicality, resourcefulness and other distinctively American qualities that he brought from his culture. Cases could be multiplied indefinitely. It has become common for generous, young Americans to dedicate some years of their lives after graduation to service in third world countries. If they return home viewing the world with the same attitudes and priorities they took with them when they left, their service was probably not very useful, but what in fact happens is that they are changed as well as the people they have lived amongst. It may well be that the transformation effected in the volunteers is the most important result of the project. These examples are secular but there is no clear dividing line between what is secular and what is sacred in a culture. The more affective and imaginative temperament of those Mexican peasants; their closeness to nature and preference for the human over the technological; their more contemplative than activist bent: all of these characteristics come to expression in their prayer, their liturgy, their understanding and practice of the gospel, and those accustomed to a more cerebral and pragmatic tradition can be delivered from undue rigidity and inhibition in our spirituality by contact with them. The earthiness of simple agricultural peoples in their prayer and worship can humanize the spirituality of the more sophisticated and, on the other hand, the intellectual approach of highly educated Christians can protect popular religion against superstition. We can all profit from contact with our opposites in matters of religion and otherwise.

The more a religious community is locked into these cultural peculiarities of any people, the less capable it is of being a world church, an instrument for drawing the whole human family into a common project with the one Saviour of all. It takes the influence of many peoples and cultures, actively affecting each other, to break open the community and to prevent it from solidifying in one form. The more religion is seen as permeating every corner of life, the more important this cultural interchange becomes. If the task of Christianity could be confined to certain ritual acts or even to the observance of a definite set of regulations, one cultural pattern might conceivably serve for all peoples (though even in this case, the same externals would receive very different interpretations), but nothing could be more foreign to Christian faith than such a limitation. Christian faith can accept nothing less that the whole of life, personal and social, as the arena for its action, and for such a mission it must be flexible enough to adapt to every culture where it finds itself, not reducing them to sameness, after the image of the melting pot, but keeping them in lively interaction with each other.

No doubt this sounds utopian and far removed from the actualities of the world we experience. Religious groups are often more provincial than secular ones. Practically speaking how much influence does a local parish receive from outside its own membership, which is often fairly homogeneous in terms of social class, nationality, etc.? How much of the vast and diverse tradition of the church is channelled to the ordinary congregation? More, I suspect, than appears at first sight. Picture the local community as the innermost of a series of concentric circles, each enclosed within a larger circle in a series which stretches as far as you can see. The circles are not sealed off from each other. There is an ebb and flow, an interchange between them in many informal ways. The picture corresponds to the situation where local churches are in communion with each other and form part of one universal communion of Christians. "Communion" here does not mean that each local church is in actual contact with all the rest. The world is too vast and local churches too limited and too short-lived for that. It is sufficient that individual Christians and local churches acknowledge that they are not self-contained and self-sufficient; they cannot go their own way, independently of the rest, because their fellowship with all other Christians belongs to the essence of their identity as Christians. When communion of this sort exists, actual influence can take place as needed.

What I have been discussing is the juridical ideal of communion, but when the juridical ideal is recognized, tangible effects occur in many little ways. The local leader may come from a very different background; the communicants may be strangers, but because there is an acceptance in faith that the church is universal, strangers are welcomed and the ministry of the ordained leader is recognized, however unfamiliar his features and style. True, the welcome is often shamefully imperfect but there is an underlying acknowledgment that, given essential faith, all do belong, and the strangers in turn are aware that however much they may be excluded from other societies, in the church of Jesus Christ they are at home by right and not by sufferance. They bring with them more than passive presence. In many unsuspected ways they are a leaven, resisting the tendency of the local congregation to settle into complacency. These lines are being written in the very cosmopolitan city of Toronto. Joining in a Catholic liturgy in a Toronto city parish, where one will be sharing the Eucharist with people of many continents and nations, is evidence that universality is real and tangible. It cannot fail to effect change and growth in all who are involved.

What I have been describing is a generalized cultural diversity, which necessarily affects the church, but there is also a particular religious diversity, which is especially important for dialogue within the Christian community. Religion itself is not monochromatic. There is no one type of "religious" personality, rather as evidenced in the various world religions, different strands enter into religious experience: prophetic, priestly, mystic and ethical, and different roles develop to service those distinctive aspects. No doubt it is their own type of personality which attracts some to one role and others to another, but exercising a particular function within the community will in turn mark the personality and shape the sensitivities and thought pattern of those who render that type of service.

Priests (in any tradition) usually have different priorities than prophets. As the man or woman charged with worship and ritual, the priest will regularly put high priority on religious ceremonial. Confrontation with public authorities who can abolish or at least hinder the free exercise of religion will appear to the priest as a danger to be avoided at almost any cost, not necessarily out of fear of persecution, which he has in common with the rest of Christians, but because he sincerely values sacramental life most highly. Prophets and reformers, on the other hand, may recognize an injustice or abuse with such clarity and passion that all other considerations appear secondary. The theologian may be so fascinated by a discovery she has made after an enormous investment of time and effort that she cannot comprehend the reluctance of others to reevaluate accepted practices in its light. Pastors will tend to be so preoccupied with the effect of a decision on ordinary people that less immediate but ultimately more important considerations will be ignored.

And thinking not only of individual charisms but also of wider traditions with their own characteristic emphasis, the awe and mystery of a liturgy celebrated incolorful vestments amid clouds of incense and elaborate ceremonial in eastern Christian rites will seem artificial and perhaps inauthentic to Christians listening to the word of God with great responsiveness in a plain Quaker meeting hall but that elaborate ritual has something to say—and more importantly to do—for Christians of a different orientation just as the unadorned service of the word in that meeting hall supplies a dimension of Christian living which can be lost in more mystical and sacramental traditions.

In all cases thetemptation is to take the easy way out, avoiding the painful confrontation that often accompanies dialogue, by letting each party go its separate way unobstructed (and uncorrected) by the other. But the easy way is not the healthy way and dialogue will only be avoided at the expense of genuine catholicity. Finally remember that the dialogue I have in mind here is not simply academic discussion but dialogue according to the expanded definition introduced earlier, which consists in *conviviality* in the original meaning of that word: a "living together," an undivided community, where in spite of diversity and certainly not without tension, people remain in interactive contact with each other.

Ideology or Community

In the final section of this chapter I would like to face up to the most serious objection which can be raised against the thesis of this whole book.. It derives from the nature ofthe dialectical process which we have been praising. Simply stated the objection is that no claim to secure and permanent truth can survive the dialectical process. All is swallowed up in relativism, the foundations of the Christian faith no less than any other purportedly changeless truth. First I propose to examine this objection on the level of logic. As such what we are saying may appear to be a philosophical digression but the objection is too crucial to be ignored and more significantly still, it can only be answered by drawing attention to an aspect of Christianity which is central to the argument of this book and indispensable for Christian faith, though it is in danger of being overlooked today.

Dialectical process is three pronged. It begins with an affirmation (thesis); something is proposed as true. The affirmation necessarily calls forth a denial or negation (antithesis). The struggle between the two is resolved by a new forward step (synthesis) in the ascent to truth, which goes beyond each of the originial positions taken separately; their opposition is overcome as each contributes its measure of truth, now modified by the other. The synthesis newly achieved reigns for a while, but it too must be denied or contested, since it does not contain the whole truth, and out of the contestation a new synthesis will emerge, only to suffer the same fate as its predecessor. Knowledge becomes a process rather than an acquisition.

It is evident how much light the discovery of the dialectical pattern has cast on the history of thought, or perhaps I might better say on the historical character of thinking. Thinking does not take place in a vacuum; it is inevitably a response to a challenge and this is as true in matters of religion as in matters of politics. The catalyst for progress in religious thought, the agency responsible for the development of doctrine is the dialectical process. The Christian community formulated dogmas because of a contemporary need. Since the dogmas were necessarily partial expressions of faith, they provoked a response in the name of those other sides of the truth which were left out, then out of the interaction, new more subtle expression and understanding resulted. And what we have said of dogma, which is the most authoritative level of church teaching, is a true *a fortiori* of less fundamental forms of teaching and practice.

So much for the positive side of dialectic; let us turn our attention to the threat it poses—some would say—to any absolute and permanent truth and consequently to any universal claims made for the Christian religion. Essentially the objection is that, according to the principles of Hegelian dialectics no doctrine can be permanent and universal. Every position, every affirmation, must be negated in an endless process of dialectics and ultimately overcome and subsumed in a new synthesis. No particular truth can be final and absolute. And so if the Christian religion is seen as having any definite form, any consistent body of doctrine, it cannot be a permanent home for all humanity but only a station along the way, albeit a beautiful and important one. Catholicity becomes an impossible ideal. Only the process is absolute; whatever is particular—and Christian religion is inescapably particular—is dissolved in that endless process.

From the standpoint of logic, the simplest answer to this objection is that it turns a very useful but partial insight into the thinking process into an absolute norm for judging all reality. Dialectical process is a tool for understanding how the advance of learning takes place; it is not a complete explanation and when treated as such it is self-contradictory. Philosophical principles are relativized in the name of what is itself a philosophical principle. If dialectical method undermines any absolute claim to truth, then dialectical method is itself subverted. Either the dialectical philosophy is an exception to the rule that all propositions are negated by their contraries and swallowed up in a new synthesis and thereby it refutes itself, or it is one more partial and passing step in the progress toward greater wisdom and thereby forfeits the right to judge other truth claims. To borrow an expression from Peter Berger, it is necessary to "relativize the relativizers." In other words, it is thoroughly illogical to argue to the relativity of all propositions on the basis of one proposition treated as an absolute.

Every statement presupposes the existence of absolute truth (even the statement that no absolute truth exists!) At the very least it presupposes that there is a difference between what is asserted and its contrary, otherwise the statement would be not so much false as meaningless and all human thought and language would be worthless. Therefore, to come to the essential point I am making, dialectical process does not exclude permanent and changeless truth, though it does restrict its ambience in a salutary way. It alerts us to an element of relativity and change, mingled with the most certain assertion, but it does not deny a core of absolute truth which is not dissolved in the three pronged process we described above. The initial statement is not *totally* denied in the second prong. It may contain an irreducible element of truth, set in a matrix which is historically conditioned. It is the historically conditioned matrix which is corrected without necessarily obliterating the initial statement. There are, I propose, absolute truths, metaphysical principles, which survive the dialectical process. I would argue further that there are propositions which are unconditionally and universally true, although they are few in number and extremely difficult, if not impossible, to formulate and the language in which they are expressed does not enjoy the same absolute quality as the truths themselves. This last point needs to be emphasized. The core of absolute and unchanging truth must not be identified with any set of words. Truth is not the same as its expression in words, images and concepts; the latter are certainly more contingent and more time conditioned than the former, and although I made the claim earlier that there were propositions which are unconditionally and universally true, the case for absolute truth does not stand or fall with this claim. If one were unable to produce a single example of a proposition which is finally and incontestably true, this would not prove that absolute truth does not exist but only that human language is always inadequate to express it. Here we touch upon something which is critically important for the argument of this book. That the church is catholic means taht it has something to offer all mankind of all ages, something which is never out of date, never bypassed in any dialectical process. What it has to offer, then, is not simply a document, by which I mean the physical reality of a book—lines written in ink on paper—because the writing does not *mean* anything until it is interpreted, and it will not yield the same meaning to different persons approaching it with different questions and from different standpoints. Therefore, the document alone cannot found a commonality for its readers. The most obvious limitation of any document is that it must be written in a particular language, hence the majority of humanity will be dependent on a translation (itself always an interpretation) to discover any meaning, and even for the minority who know the language of the document, different interpretations are possible. No writings, therefore, taken by themselves alone, even the inspired writings of the Bible, can provide grounding for a universal church.

The objection we have just been considering feeds into a more vague, less logically reasoned objection, similar in outline to that discussed above but so much more widespread that it often seems to be a common-place assumption. We have touched upon aspects of it earlier but it is important enough to deserve more direct and thorough attention. Put most simply, it is the belief that no religion can be universal. We must accept the fact—so the objection goes—that all religions are partial responses to the mystery of existence. None of them can credibly sustain the claim to the THE true faith and the one church for all mankind. Why not admit that there are many different paths to God, each with its own strengths and weaknesses? Let each religious family treasure and perfect its own tradition while respecting others and abandon all designs for conversion. Granted that at the earliest levels of Christian faith, represented by the Gospels and other New Testament writings, universal claims were made for Christ and for his church, doesn't this belong to a primitive stage of development, understandable enough from the standpoint of the first century but incredible to one living in the twentieth century? Those early Christians knew almost nothing of the far east or of the continents of North and South America or even of the wider ranges of Europe and Africa. They were certainly unaware of the great civilizations, replete with their own wisdom and lofty morality, that had flourished for centuries in China and India. Can anyone today believe that all of these people were "lost," because they had no contact, as far as we can discern, with the God who revealed himself in Israel and in Jesus Christ? Certainly the answer to that last question must be a resounding "No" and the simplest and most direct way of dealing with New Testament texts which affirm a unique role for Jesus and a universal mission for his church is to abandon them as obsolete. The objection is seductive and it has seduced many, many Christians included.

Yet it does collide with the bedrock of Christian faith. Jesus Christ is not one among many great religious teachers, whose wisdom has illuminated our human journey. He is the Incarnate Son of God and the saviour of the whole world. It is not primarily by teaching us but by joining us to himself in his death and resurrection that he becomes our way to the Father. The saving event of Calvary renewed in the Eucharist stands at the center of all history and only that which somehow passes through this center becomes part of the one plan of salvation. Such is the non-negotiable core of Christian faith. To abandon this claim to uniqueness and even to exclusivity is to surrender the substance of Christian faith. It may also be to surrender the most timely thing Christians have to say to the world of the twentieth century, and the one which responds most immediately to the felt needs of the secular world, because claiming a unique and universal role for Jesus is at the same time and necessarily affirming a radical unity of all humanity inspite of the surface differences and hostilities that threaten to destroy us, and affirming that common unity not in terms of some airy and abstract ideal but on the deepest level of human motivation, rooted in religious faith. If all mankind was created with a common destiny and the fate of each person and each people is connected with that of all the rest—and this is necessarily implied in the Christian dogma of Jesus as Savior and Redeemer of all, who calls all to join him in the same kingdom—then political efforts to unify the family of nations, which secular thinkers recognize as a critical need today, are consistent with and a continuation of God's own plan for humanity. In a world living under the shadow of nuclear holocaust, even agnostics and secularists cannot afford to pass up that kind of assistance coming from religion.

Let me add a word of caution here lest I seem to be defending a naive and simplistic interpretation of Christ's salvation and his church's mission. We have come a long way from the sixteenth century understanding of mission, when other world religions and the wisdom and culture of unevangelized peoples could be treated as error and superstition to be eradicated and supplanted by Christianity. Moreover, we ought to reject out of hand any suggestion that eternal salvation is only possible for those who have heard and accepted the explicit teaching of the gospel and been baptized into formal membership within the Christian community. Such a view is simply indefensible. Christ did not come to destroy what God had done before his birth, especially in Israel but also throughout the world and from the beginning of history. He came to fulfill all of it. If the role Jesus performs in the history of mankind is universal in its influence—and Christian faith asserts that it is—that role does not consist in supplanting every other but in completing everything else which is true and good and gathering it into a convergence which leads through him to the Father in the Spirit.

The Second Vatican Council put this clearly when it affirmed that, "the Catholic Church rejects nothing of what is true and holy in these (non-Christian) religions...(which) often reflect a ray of that truth which enlightens all men." But it goes on to add "Yet she proclaims and is in duty bound to proclaim without fail, Christ who is the way, the truth and the life

(Jn. 14:6). In him, in whom God reconciled all things to himself (2 Cor.5:18,19), men find the fullness of their religious life."[9] It is this latter point that I want to insist on here. The universality of the church must be conceived in an inclusive rather than exclusive fashion, as we have been arguing throughout this book. Linkage with Christ and with his church in Holy Spirit can be invisible and unsuspected but this linkage is essential. How concretely it is achieved is a question we do not intend to address here. It is enough to reaffirm with the New Testament and the continuing Christian tradition that Jesus Christ is the Savior of all mankind and that his church has correspondingly a mission to all.

A defense of the uniqueness and universality of Jesus Christ and of the church which extends his presence and mission, rests upon two pillars, both of which are in danger of being overlooked. The first is the dogma of the Incarnation. Jesus Christ is truly God as well as man. In the flesh and blood reality of this man from Nazareth the infinite and eternal God makes contact with our world. If this cornerstone of faith is denied or forgotten any claim to universality becomes absurdly pretentious. If all religions are human efforts to reach the transcendent God, they are all essentially equal. Some may be nobler than others but there is nothing to ground a claim to real uniqueness and universality and no justification for a mission to all humanity.

The second pillar on which the claim to a universal mission for the Christian church rests ties in more directly with the theme of this chapter. Without agreeing that dialectics undercuts any permanently valid principles and any propositions which are unconditionally and universally true, which we have maintained is an extreme and even self-contradictory extension of dialectical method, it can be successfully argued, I believe, that no system of thought, no integrated body of teaching, no philosophy, can be so permanently and universally valid that it could serve as a foundation for catholicity. Systems of thought are useful only for a limited time and within a limited scope not everywhere and always. If Christianity were an ideology—the word is used loosely, postponing more careful analysis until later—it could not be catholic.

Thought, language, ideas are secondary and derivative, not primary. They derive from reality. It is true that once formed they in turn influence the reality from which they originate (as we pointed out in chapter two) but being is first, thought follows. The language and ideas whereby people understand reality are always partly subjective. They describe and explain the real as it appears from a particular standpoint and not in pure objectivity. They are the product of this particular people and as such are shaped by its peculiarities. Underlying the differences, humanity does grasp some universal and absolute truth but when there is question of a complete philosophy, an integrated system of explanation, what we may call for want of a better name, an ideology, subjective factors are such that no one such ideology can be catholic. Human experience is too diverse to permit it. Thought has a *history*. The process cannot be arrested at any privileged moment so that the understanding, the ideology, of that time and place becomes a fixed and final norm, made definitive for all humanity. The whole human family can never be gathered into one ideology; if the church of Jesus Christ is capable of gathering all into its unity (and that is what catholicity means) it must be because it is not an ideology.

The center, the core, the foundation of the Christian religion is not an idea but a reality. Let me specify further. Christianity is based upon a real, historical person, Jesus of Nazareth, not upon an understanding of him, which is always imperfect and may be widely diverse; nor even upon faith in him, because faith is a response on the part of a believer to the person, and a response is secondary and dependent on the reality it responds to. Faith is, of course, utterly fundamental to the Christian. Without it there would have been no incentive to gather the facts about this person and to interpret them, and then or now no one can enter a vital relationship with Jesus without faith, but the point is that even faith is not the ground level, the bottom rung of Christianity. The absolute beginning is Jesus of Nazareth himself, however he is understood.

What is being said here is not itself a judgement of faith. How one interprets and evaluates the person of Jesus is indeed a judgement of faith but it seems to me that to affirm that the Christian religion is ultimately founded on the existential reality of Jesus himself is nothing but a neutral, historical judgement that could be made by anyone, believer or not, who is moderately acquainted with the facts. Christianity like Judaism is an historical religion, which means that it is a belief about historical happenings. If this belief is wrong, it is wrong about history not about eternal truths or abstract ideas.

To fill out a little more the point we have been making, Jesus is the foundation of Christian faith not passively like a statue or a sacred fixed point but in the complete expression of his personality, which is co-extensive with the whole of his life: his words and deeds and especially his death and resurrection. To put it briefly, what forms the base supporting the entire edifice of Christianity is the "Jesus *event*." We are not, therefore, downgrading the importance of Jesus' teaching—teaching is uniquely important in Christian religion—but his teaching does not stand by itself, apart from his person and his life, as teaching ordinarily does. Jesus was no moral philosopher. He taught about the kingdom of God, which is not an abstract idea, but a real intervention of God in our world, concretized in the living person of Jesus of Nazareth. To be a Christian is not to agree with some theoretical reflections expressed by Jesus but more radically to be part of his company, to be joined with him in a common project taking place in history.

I have risked being repetitious in underlining the theme of this section because it has such momentous implications for the catholicity of the church. If Jesus himself in person is the pivot on which catholicity swings, much ambiguity can be accepted within the circle which radiates out from him. Misunderstanding and infidelity are of course regrettable but they do not cancel out all relationship to a real person, and even the most accurate and orthodox understanding is incomplete. If it is true that our minds never exhaust the richness of any event, and that each succeeding age can discover more meaning in it than its predecessor did, how much truer this is for the most significant event of all time? I can be associated with a person whom I understand imperfectly or even defectively. If an accurate understanding of Jesus were the minimal requisite for linkage with him, the boundaries of the church would be narrow, but if it is Jesus himself and not our knowledge of him and adherence to his message that constitutes the deepest foundation of Christianity, then we can speak meaningfully of "anonymous Christians," who are vitally united to the risen Jesus, even though they have no explicit knowledge of him and we can recognize as sharing in the communion of Christian life those whose theology is erroneous and whose practice of Christian virtues is deficient. To be sure, Christians will appreciate that it is critically important to grow in knowledge, love and imitation of Jesus and they will recognize a corporate responsibility of the company of believers to purify itself and foster that growth in each other, but they will also acknowledge that the process admits of endless degrees and they will not disregard even the earliest and most faltering steps along the way.

As Jesus himself in person is the center of the whole Christian religion so the community is the extension of Jesus in the world—not the ideas or even the faith of the community but the community in itself, in its own existential reality. Of course it is faith which draws this community together; without faith it would have no reason to exist, but as we observed that the message of Jesus is grounded in the prior reality of his person and his work, so the faith of the church is grounded in its real, historical existence as a body of men and women, journeying together through the centuries, with the risen Jesus in their midst and the Holy Spirit breathing life into their fellowship. The sequence here is logical rather than chronological. The church does not exist first, and then subsequently its faith and institutions. They are inseparable, but being is logically prior to thought and the same very significant implications we derive from this principle is the case of Jesus himself, apply, *mutatis mutandis,* to the church community.

We have argued that an ideology cannot be catholic but a community can. An ideology cannot include its opposites, but a community can operate with much opposition inside its boundaries and be healthier for the dialogue within. The church of Christ can live with conflicting theologies, with opposing tastes, with contrasting temperments and approaches. True, there are limits to pluralism; without them the community would have no identity or purpose, but the controlling axis is not a body of teaching, taken by itself, not a theory but a living person. Doctrine can be a touchstone of membership within the community but not in itself alone; what is in question is not a system of ideas but a companionship and collaboration with a person. No doctrine and no discipline oblige the community except in so far as they emanate from and lead to Jesus. Doctrine and discipline, the external agencies of the community, flow out from the person of Jesus to bind believers together in unity and collaboration. Without them there would be no community, but it is only becasue they link us with Jesus that they have any force at all. The agencies of the community have often been misused by its officials and will continue to be so misused as long as fragile human beings are in control of them; the traveling will be bumpy with many detours, but the presence of the Holy Spirit, who extends the personal influence of Jesus through the centuries, guarantees that the essential direction will never be lost and the bond to Jesus will never be broken. Such is the faith of Christians.

If what we have said above is true, individual Christians, whether theologians or ordinary believers, ought not to overestimate the importance of their own intellectual grasp of Christian faith or their own reading of the imperatives of Christian living. This may sound like a counsel of indifference and mediocrity; saints and martyrs have sacrificed their lives rather than compromise that they saw as orthodox doctrine or their own personal vocation. They were right in doing so, but what has been said above still stands. In asserting that the real center of faith is not a teaching but a person, not a body of doctrines and laws but a flesh and blood community, we are not minimizing the importance of doctrine and law but we are relativizing them. A person does not provide a focus for a group like an inanimate object simply by its physical existence, but by personal communication, by language, thought and love, by the actions which tell his followers who he is. Similarly a human community does not gather its members into fellowship and collaboration like a swarm of bees but by all the language, formal and informal, where by human life is shared on the level of human personality. Doctrine, then, and obedience can be overwhelmingly important in so far as they are a expression of and a connection with Jesus himself and his body, which is the church. It is by means of teaching, rituals and institutions that the risen Christ extends his invisible, spiritual influence into the whole fabric of our lives, therefore they participate, in varying degrees, in his own unconditional importance.

There is always a danger, though, that formulas of belief and rules of practice, intellectual insights and personal convictions, the expressions of our own individual grasp of the Christian message may become disconnected from the reality which gives them meaning. We can be attached to them in themselves, since they are, after all, our own. Occasions may arise where intellectual honesty requires a person to sever his connection with the community of Christians, but anyone who keeps in mind what we have been saying here will be suspicious of any individual insight, however compelling, which separates him from the living, existential reality of the church. Reality is richer than ideas; gradually ideas catch up with it, but the substance of Christian life and faith lies deeper than any ideas. It lies in the real person of the Son of God, who "pitched his tent among us"[10] in the very tangible world we inhabit and now, risen from the dead, is still touching not only our minds but our whole human reality through the social body, which in spite of its blemishes, he has joined to himself and vivified with his own Spirit.

We have been contrasting community with ideology. It is time to examine the latter more closely. The name has become associated with a Marxist analysis of society, but it is used here in a more neutral and general sense. Fundamental to the notion of ideology is that it is a system of ideas, a concentration of assumptions, procedures, judgements, explanations, a way of thinking which exists to justify and defend the society which created it, rather than as a neutral and disinterested effort to find the truth for its own sake alone. Must we not grant that every philosophy and every theology, like every economic and political theory has elements of ideology within it? Thought does not exist for its own sake but for the sake of life. Thinking is part of life and it is subordinated to the overall purposes of living. We think about and try to explain what we experience and we use our intellectual picture of the world we know to guide that world and to protect the values we cherish within it. There is no need to exaggerate; if the explanation and evaluation are purely utilitarian, if, that is, they support uncritically the world they are trying to explain, they will serve it badly. Any honest thinker will be drawn at the same time and in some measure to discover the truth whatever its consequences, so pure ideology is rare. But pure objectivity is rarer still.

The conclusion is, as we stated earlier, that ideology cannot be catholic, or to approach from the opposite direction, the church of Jesus Christ can be catholic because it is not an ideology but a community. To be sure ideologies are found within the church. I would argue that ideology is a universal human need and that there is nothing nefarious about it on two conditions, first that we are alert to the danger inherent in ideology of absolutizing our own norms of judgement, that is treating our own norms of judgement as identical with pure and simple truth, and second that we are open-minded and receptive to truth which does not fit into our ideology. Ideology is useful as a framework to organize our knowledge but it can function like a pair of blinders restricting our vision. If our minds and hearts are free, the gospel and God's continuing action on our world will lead us beyond our ideologies. There are many ideological aspects within the theologies. There are many ideological aspects within the theologies, scriptural interpretations and cultural patterns within the church, but the church herself is not commited to any of them. They belong to her, not she to them, and she can modify or shed them when their usefulness is past.

In one of his poesm T.S. Eliot speaks of "the point of intersection of the timeless with time."[11] It occurs to me that this is an apt description of the church of Jesus Christ. She is the point where the infinite and eternal God meets historical mankind. The meeting is actual, not imaginary. A point is real and particular, not a theory or ideology. If she were a detailed figure much would have to remain outside because it did not fit into the determined shape, but because she is a point there is no limit to what she can gather around herself and permeate with the divine life which flows into the world through her. She does not remain a solitary point but with unlimited magnetic force draws upon all that is around her. What acquires a permanent place within her does so not because of its own distinctive form but because of its relation to that one point and center, the Incarnation of God in our world.

Is this an invitation to doctrinal indifference? Does it turn Christianity into an amorphous paste which can be molded into any shape around the center which is Jesus Christ? Certainly not. There are changeless articles of faith. There are nonnegotiable structures. What I am suggesting is a question of perspective. Let me illustrate again by the metaphor of a wheel. The point or hub would not be in contact with its surroundings without the spokes which radiate out from it, but the spokes are useless and even harmful when broken off from the axis (the axis, according to my metaphor, being the risen Jesus, and the spokes those dogmas, practices and forms which mediate his presence to us). The power and durability of the axis is not present equally in every sector of the spokes, but in diminishing force as they emanate from the center. So the closer any element within the Christian community, doctrine, sacrament, law or whatever, is to the core of Christian faith and life, namely Jesus himself, in the mystery of his life, death and resurrection, the more indispensable that element will be; likewise, the further removed the more it will be subject to change and revision. What must be insisted on above all is that the only source of permanence and efficacy is that linkage to the center, which is not an ideology, not a body of teaching or an inspiration but a living, concrete person, present not as an idea in our minds but in the concrete reality of human history.

Notes

1. Monika Hellwig, *Tradition: The Catholic Story Today* (Dayton, Ohio: Pflaum Press, 1974), Chapter Two.

2. 1 Cor. 10:16,17.

3. See especially Jerome Hamer, *O.p., The Church Is A Communion* (London: Geoffrey Chapman, 1964).

4. Rom. 5:18.

5. The observation made here briefly is developed with great insight by William F. Lynch, S.J. in a book entitled, *Images Of Hope: Imagination As Healer Of The Hopeless* (Notre Dame, Ind: University of Notre Dame, 1974) also in other works of Lynch, especially, *Christ And Apollo: The Dimensions Of The Literary Imagination* (N.Y.: New American Library: Mentor—Omega Book, 1963). In fact, anyone interested in a much deeper development of the themes in this book will find great profit in all Lynch's difficult but rewarding books.

6. *The Analogical Imagination: Christian Theology And The Thought* (N.Y.: Crossroad, 1981).

7. *The Integrating Mind: An Exploration Into Western Thought* (N.Y.: Sheed and Ward, 1962).

8. See 1 Cor. 12:3-8.

9. Declaration on the Relation of the Church to Non-Christian Religious (Nostra Aetate) Oct. 28, 1965, trans., Fr. Killian, O.S.C.O. in Documents of Vatican II, Austin P. Flannery, ed. (Grand Rapids, MI: Erdmans, 1975) p. 739.

10. Jn. 1:14.

11. "The Dry Salvages" from "Four Quartets," *Complete Poems And Plays Of T.s. Eliot.* (London: Faber & Faber, 1969), p. 189.

Chapter Four

Catholicity vs. Sectarianism: Some Samples

It is time to take stock of where we have been and where we are going. The one central theme of this whole book is that the church of Jesus Christ must be catholic. Now as never before, it is only by being catholic, that the church can carry out the mission she has received from her master. If "God is one (and) one also is the mediator between God and men, the man Christ Jesus, who gave himself as a ransom for all,"[1] then the church was catholic in principle and potentiality from Calvary on, and it seems obvious and banal to say she must be catholic now, but the commission and the radical power to gather in all humanity is one thing and the fulfillment of that commission is another. Progress toward fulfilling the commission is not a steady incline but a winding and uneven road with an occasional sharp climb. There are plateaus when the route is plane and the traveling relatively uneventful, but we are presently at the foot of a steep ascent.

Decisive moments occur when the church breaks free of one cultural mold and enters a period of dramatic growth, not necessarily numerical—it might even be accompanied by numerical decline—but internal growth, growth in the capacity to assimilate new peoples and new cultures. This she does by shedding what is no longer appropriate—always a difficult and painful process, never achieved without losses—and reaching out to new human realities not previously impregnated by the Gospel.

If the great German theologian, Karl Rahner, is correct, the Second Vatican Council represents such a decisive moment, so decisive, in fact, that it would be necessary to go back to the first century to find a parallel.[2] Then the infant church was called out of the closed Jewish world where it was born and became an integral part of the Greco-Roman culture out of which our modern western civilization has sprung. How difficult that first great transition was is evident enough in the New Testament. Through the intervening centuries the community gathered in the name of Jesus has passed many milestones along the road to becoming not one sect among others but a church for the whole human family, and the agency through which God is realizing his one great plan of bringing "All things in the heavens and on earth into one under Christ's headship."[3] New continents have been converted as in the case of North and South America. Revolutions, political, social and intellectual, have been confronted and then partially assimilated, but none of these events, according to Rahner, matches in importance the thrust for catholicity in our own day.

Since she emerged from the womb of Judaism, the Christian church has been largely identified with that culture which it first purified and baptized, the Greco-Roman, classical civilization, later extended into modern Europe and exported—changed and Christianized but essentially the same—to other continents. With the Second Vatican Council, Rahner suggests, the Church has begun to be a church for the whole world and not only for the west.

What we are concerned about in the process whereby the church of Jesus Christ, which was catholic in principle from its beginning and of its very nature, becomes catholic or universal, in fact is less the external expansion than the internal changes which are both the condition for and the result of meaningful expansion. A building can only be enlarged if its own internal structures are broad enough to support the addition. Even more, an organism cannot enjoy healthy growth unless its present state is adapted to receiving the growth. It is true that the two movements, external expansion and internal adaptation, mutually influence each other and cannot happen separately, but for us, the spotlight is on the internal adaptation. To pick up the language of our first chapter, it is not so much catholicity of persons we are interested in, for that is obvious, but a catholicity of the total cultural matrix in which believers live. People do not exist alone but in constant intercourse with the world around them—the material world and the human world, with its institutions and expectations, its patterns of living and acting. If that larger cultural matrix is unaffected, baptizing the individuals who live within it will not make the church adequately catholic.

The call to breadth, to openness, to genuine universality can be looked at in two different ways. It can be seen as a duty which weighs upon the church as an institution, and therefore most especially upon its pastors and others in positions of leadership, to innovate and be expansive and open minded before the unprecedented opportunities of our time. But it is equally important to see it from another angle, too. It is not just that the church as an institution needs to be catholic to survive and be vital; it is also true that we individual Christians need a church which is catholic for the sake of our own individual Christian vocation. Christianity without the dimension of universality is defective Christianity for our times. The church needs to be catholic; but we individual believers need the church in order to be what the *kairos*—the peculiar circumstances in which God has placed us and which therefore reveal his special will for us—require us to be. An individualistic religion will not do. To take refuge in a private and strictly personal religion, to give up on the church community and to accept the bounds of our own individual religious experience or of a closed group which satisfies our emotional needs, as the limits of our religious life, is not only unwise tactically, in terms of our own spiritual life, but it is a betrayal of our vocation as Christians at this historic moment. It has never been more essential than now that Christian life be ecclesial rather than individualistic. The church as community has never been more indispensable to Christian existence. Such was the burden of our second chapter, but allow me to recall and expand on it a little here, for it seems to me an important but often forgotten truth.

Sectarian Christianity can satisfy many individuals, perhaps more now than ever before, but it is not equal to the needs of our time and it is only by diminishing our humanity, by blocking out much of the data which as contemporary men and women we ought to face, that we can buy such satisfaction. To seek it is to betray our collective vocation as Christians at this moment in history. Is there a contradiction here? Our times demand a Christianity which is as wide as the world, but narrow, sectarian Christianity seems to be growing in appeal, while the more catholic forms of Christian belief decline; it is the sectarian type of Christian living which seems most satisfying to many people today. I do not believe there is any contradiction. Christianity is not first and foremost in the business of providing satisfaction; often in fact, with Christians as with the prophets of the Old Testament, a sign of authenticity is that the message offered is not the one people want to hear. Then, too, satisfaction can be short lived and deceptive. We have argued that the challenges to Christian faith and Christian life can only be met effectively by a community, not by individuals acting alone; they are too many and too diverse to be matched by the resources of the individual. The individual can find a refuge but only by refusing to come to grips with the challenges or worse still by confining the Christian within him to acts of devotion and the sphere of private morality, leaving the great public issues to be solved without reference to faith. Keep in mind that the summons to catholicity discussed above is not exclusively geographical or even broadly cultural, as though it only concerned new contact between Christian believers and other large groups, previously out of range. The pluralism of our twentieth century world touches every individual, at least to the extent that he or she does not withdraw into seclusion. It is as close as the nearest television set or newspaper. The barriers that used to protect some groups and places within a secure and traditional Christianity have almost all fallen. When the problem is so overwhelmingly social, no individualistic answer is adequate.

In the last chapter we have explored how a community must function in order to be catholic, and we found the key in dialogue, stretching that overused word in many directions. To be catholic the community must be open. It must never cut off debate on anything not strictly essential to its life and function; it must not be finally wedded to any style or practice, to any institution or cultural form that is not necessary to its very identity. It must resist the tendency in all groups to solidify in its ways and become complacent. It must welcome the demand for change as long as it is coupled with fundamental loyalty. It must tolerate the frustrations and antagonisms which are inescapable when people of widely different temperament and background work together. Clearly to live up to these ideals, the community will require more than human resources and even with the constant guidance of the Holy Spirit we will have to settle for imperfect success until the Lord comes again!

So far we have been dealing mostly in generalities; in this chapter I want to get down to particulars. Let me begin by mapping out where we plan to go. First, I shall propose a test for catholicity and then proceed to apply that test to three major areas of Christian faith.

If one word can stand as a criterion for catholicity, it is the word *openness*. We have discussed this at some length earlier but it will help to focus our exploration into catholicity in the concrete, if we highlight here what that openness entails. There are two ways you can approach anything; one is closed, the other open; one is exclusive, the other inclusive. You can concentrate on it and block out everything else or you can see it as a part of a larger whole. The former is sectarian, the latter catholic. That a vision is partial does not make it sectarian. All visions are partial. It is sectarian if the part is cut off from the whole. The whole is not an enemy of the part but its completion and the kind of wholeness which would dissolve its parts into a shapeless mixture is not human wholeness. Without concentration nothing would be accomplished and the individual must resign himself to partiality, leaving fullness and perfect balance to the community. Still concentration on one part need not deny others nor pretend to completeness; it can leave room for light coming from other directions. The openness we are praising as the essence of catholicity is not opposed to particularity but only to exclusiveness. It recognizes that we must have our own particular place to live but it requires doors and windows rather than solid walls. Catholicity is openness to diversity, even to opposition. Faced with alternatives, the catholic tendency is to affirm both rather than choose between them. It is willing to forego the pleasures of closure, of finality and to live with the provisional. This is itself an act of faith that the purposes it serves are larger than those it understands and that its welfare and its mission are in the hands of Someone who does not fit inside our minds and imaginations.

A Catholic Bible

Christian faith is nourished first of all by the Sacred Scriptures so it is appropriate to begin there. There are two ways of dealing with God's inspired word, the Bible; one is sectarian the other catholic. My contention is that only the catholic way is intellectually responsible in our time. This may seem contentious and even uncharitable and so it is important to clarify what is being said. What is at issue is objective not subjective responsibility. Any acknowledgment of the deep conviction and genuine holiness to be found among Christians who use the Bible in sectarian fashion would be absurdly patronizing. It is too evident to deserve mention. Yet is should be said, I believe, that a sectarian approach does not do justice to the gift God has given us in his written word. Moreover, it presents to educated women and men of our day a vision of faith and a spirituality which they cannot accept without compromising the intellectual heritage they possess simply because they do belong, integrally and not peripherally, to the late twentieth century. Make no mistake about it, confronted by a choice between twentieth century culture and Christian faith, I have no doubt that it is Christian faith which should be chosen, but God does not ask us to make such a choice. He offers his message to every culture and to ignore what has been learned by secular means is to refuse light which comes from God, not the brightest light he has offered us, but nonetheless light that has its source in him. The individual who embraces the faith of Jesus in a cultural form ill suited to her own world will be immeasurably enriched personally by it but she will be weighted down with unnecessary burdens and worse still the sharing of these riches with her contemporaries will be gravely hindered.

It has always been true that the sacred scriptures exercise their power most effectively if they are used in a catholic way, and it was in this catholic way that the great body of Christians used them from the beginning but in our own time the reasons for a catholic approach to the Bible have multiplied. This is what I shall be trying to prove in the pages which follow.

To use the Bible in a catholic way is to be open to the whole of the Bible and to all the dimensions of its many sided reality. To use the Bible in a sectarian way is to focus on some parts and to forget others, whether the parts in question be whole books, or more subtly, the angle of vision or the approach to what is written. As always catholicity means openness to the whole; sectarianism is narrow and partial; it is tunnel vision, riveted to one segment of the truth, dislocated from its wider context.

The first sectarian temptation in dealing with the Bible is to eliminate those portions which do not fit our expectations of what God ought to say. It is a temptation which goes back very far in Christian history. In the early second century Marcion, newly converted from paganism, brought his scissors to the books Christians held to be sacred and cut out the whole of the Old Testament and three of the four Gospels, because he was convinced, as many later Christians have been in less extreme form, that there was an unbridgeable gulf between the Law (here equivalent to the whole Old Testament) and the Gospel. The same God (he thought) could not be responsible for both. Marcion was giving expression to a tension which has persisted through the centuries since and is felt acutely in our own day. Do Christian love and freedom rule out any form of law and ordered institution? It would be simpler and perhaps more emotionally satisfying to opt for one side or the other; to turn Christianity into a moral code, a series of

"Do's and Don'ts," ignoring the newness of the Gospel, or to reject all law in the name of grace, but it would call for big omissions in the New as well as the Old Testament. The most lasting result of Marcion's heresy was to stimulate the church to draw up an official list of books accepted as inspired by God (the canon of sacred scripture) and in doing so to acknowledge once and for all that the Old as well as the New Testament is inspired by God and that Jesus completes and perfects rather than supplants what has gone before. By extension, the early church refused a choice between the spontaneity and infinite flexibility of grace, on the one hand, and on the other, all forms of ordered, institutionalized religious and moral practice. Grace is primary but it is not wedded to anarchy. There is a place within the Christian community, subordinate to be sure, but none the less necessary, for the external and institutional laws and structures required for the functioning of any group.

The practice of excluding from the Bible those passages which clash with one's own understanding did not die with Marcion. When Martin Luther in the sixteenth century found in the letter attributed to St. James direct contradiction to his own insight, derived, he believed, from St. Paul that justification was by faith and not by works, he concluded that the letter of James was a "letter of straw" and excluded it from the canon (or approved books) of holy scripture. It is a dramatic instance of a practice so common to Catholics and Protestants during the reformation period and its aftermath. Each side concentrated on its own preferred texts and failed to listen to the rest.

It is inevitable, of course, that each of us and each group among us will have our favorite texts. Not all the Bible is equally central nor equally relevant to everyone. Our spirituality is fed by only a fraction of the immense riches of sacred scripture. Life is too short for it to be otherwise. Catholicity consists not in hearing deeply all there is to hear but in being receptive to all, when and if, under the influence of the Holy Spirit, it is needed for our particular vocation, and above all it consists in belonging to a church that does not shut out any segment of God's word.

Openness to all parts of the Bible is only the most obvious example of a catholic approach. There are many different strains mingled in the same book and even in the same passage: prophetic, priestly, mystical, ethical, etc. Not all will appeal to us equally and there is no guarantee that those we find more appealing are those most needed or that what we pass over as unappealing is not what it is most important for us to hear.

The word of God can be treated as our servant or our master. In the former case we will attend to those passages that comfort and support us and give short shrift to the rest. Almost inevitably the isolated individual or the unconnected congregation will use the Bible in that way. But God is our master not our servant. His word is not given us as one more tool to be used for our own purposes or as a pacifier to console us when we fail to have our own way; it is to lead us in God's ways which may not be our ways, but the way of the cross and which surely transcend our limited intentions and those of our group. To believe in the divine inspiration of the scriptures is to believe that they are ultimately a voice from outside, beyond our humanity, though passing through and shaped by the human author and audience, and they must not be subordinated nor reduced to a purely human vision. To some extent the church community prevents this kind of subordination of God's word to our own designs by keeping before us the wider ranges of the scriptures, wider surely than our own tastes left to themselves would permit. I say "to some extent," because the tendency to fit God's word to our interests rather than our interests to God's word (the temptation to ideology) is at work in every agency of the church, but the more spread out over space and time the church community which mediates the scriptures to us, the more protection it offers, and when that church community is large enough to include the Holy Spirit, the hope for transcending ourselves and our group is expanded infinitely.

Not too long ago the Bible could be regarded by the ordinary believer as something given, fixed. Even translations had become stationary for centuries. (Contrast that with the number of excellent translations available at present.) It was almost as though it were a message carved in marble and coming directly from God. The text could be treated simply as it stood, without concern for the process of its coming to be. A century and a half of biblical research has dissolved that fixity. We realize that the process of composition extended over more than a thousand years, while the process of editing, not to mention that of translation, is not fully complete even now, and we are acutely aware of how much the historical setting of its composition has influenced every book of the Bible. A naive and simplistic notion of divine inspiration is hardly possible to educated people of our time. Yet as much now as ever before it is fundamental to Christian faith that the Bible—all of it—is God's book, and that in and through the human authors the Holy Spirit of God is speaking to us. The conclusion of all this must be that no passage of the Bible stands alone or can guide us wisely in God's path by itself in isolation. It must be seen in relation to the whole—the whole Bible and more, the whole background which gives it meaning. A sectarian approach riveted to the written or spoken words of the passage in question and closed to light coming from other directions will result in defective understanding of that passage and what is worse, it will substitute a purely human and perhaps ideological interpretation in place of God's word, since the interpreter is imposing his own or his society's interpretation on the biblical passage, thereby making a god after his own image—and that is a form of idolatry.

Perhaps the most striking result of recent biblical and historical studies has been the diversity it has uncovered in the Bible, especially in the New Testament and in the Christian communities where it came to birth.[4] We spoke above about different types of writing corresponding to different types of ministry and different historical situations, but the diversity goes deeper still. Such differences would be compatible with a highly unified and integrated message, delivered in different ways according to the circumstances of author and audience, and communicated not all at once but in a progressive series of revelations. It was in just such a way that God's message in the Bible was often understood, but we have learned that the plan of God is more elusive and less accessible to our minds than we imagined. There are different theologies in the Bible and different spiritualities. There is no one conceptual framework that does justice to the richness and variety of God's dealings with his people, celebrated in the holy books.

The attitude toward suffering in the Old Testament is a case in point. In the Psalms and very generally in the older books, suffering is seen as punishment for misdeeds as prosperity is the reward for fidelity to God's law. With the book of *Job* and the later part of *Isaiah* a more profound and more spiritual insight into the role of suffering in God's plan comes to light, preparing the way for the blinding new light of Calvary. There it is recognized that the earlier answer does not respond adequately to the full facts of suffering and evil. Too many innocent persons suffer grievously to attribute suffering regularly to the sins of the sufferer. Does the later vision render obsolete so much of the Old Testament? Rather both bring their own distinct contribution to our grappling with a fact too large and too obscure to fit neatly into our calculations. They do not join together like different shaped tiles in one symmetrical mosaic, but neither do they cancel each other out. They do not squeeze the facts into one conceptual framework, but they open our minds and hearts to a plan bigger than we can understand.

Turning to the New Testament we have learned that each of the four gospels has its own distinct theology and its own unique image of Jesus. It used to be thought desirable to try to harmonize all four into one consistent account, combining details from all gospels and constructing a unified biography and interpretation of Jesus. The riches and complexity of the subject matter frustrates all such projects. Each gospel has its own irreducible distinctiveness.

It is true that the earlier scepticism on the part of some biblical scholars, who felt that almost nothing could be known about the original facts of Jesus' life and teaching, has been largely abandoned with the progress of historical and critical study. When the immense labors of scientific research into the Bible and its historical background are sifted down, a solid residue of neutral, historical evidence does remain, enough to give a consistent and awesome profile of Jesus of Nazareth and of his teaching and surely enough to raise soul searching questions in the mind of any objective seeker after truth about this utterly unique person.

But this is still far short of Christian faith in Jesus and the intimate knowledge that would enable one to follow him and be joined with him in love. For this the believer must go to the gospels and once more we are thrust against their diversity. How should the believer respond to this diversity? Not by choosing one gospel perspective and excluding the others, nor by wrenching passages out of their own context and trying to hammer them into another, but by accepting their diversity as a sign of the depth and riches to which they point, a depth which can continually draw us further but which we can never exhaust, and a depth which can be fathomed incomparably more by a community than by its individual members.

What has been said of the gospels applies to the rest of the New Testament and even more to the Bible taken as a whole. One will search in vain for an outline into which the teaching of the New Testament can be fitted with logical consistency and precision. There is, for example, no ethical system which has been elaborated by the New Testament authors to guide believers in their moral choices. One can find there many directives and much moral advice but it is not systemized and thorough, so the modern Christian who tries to derive an organized and complete guide to morality from the Bible alone, is doomed to failure. The moral directives are mostly addressed to particular persons in particular circumstances; they can scarcely be transferred with simple literalness to other situations.

Added to incompleteness is diversity. What Paul has to say about ministry in the two letters to the Corinthians does not mesh perfectly with the teaching of the pastoral letters to Timothy and Titus. The vision presented in the letters of John is not identical to or simply continuous with that in the letters to the Thessalonians. Even confining attention to one author like St. Paul, there is no reason to assume that he has thought through as far as possible the various questions he addresses. It seems to me, for example, that Paul makes statements in the second chapter of *Romans* about justice and holiness among the pagans which on the surface conflict with his frequent theme that no justification is possible without faith. The contrasting statements remain like different stands which have never been knitted together into a consistent pattern. This is not to suggest that the different passages are irreconcilable; they are not. Divine inspiration does not require that the inspired author have all the answers to the questions he asks; it is sufficient that rays of light come from many directions without converging to give perfect clarity. The consequence is that a narrow and sectarian approach does not measure up to the breadth of the sacred writings.

Diversity is not the whole story, of course; underlying it there is a profound unity in the New Testament. At the very heart of Christian faith is the belief that there is only one plan of God for the whole human family and that one plan centers on Jesus of Nazareth. But the unity of the plan is a judgement of faith rather than an observation of experience and surely the pattern is not simple and obvious by human standards. In the infinite wisdom of God all human history fits into one great design but the concrete working out of the design is hidden from human eyes. If we confuse our interpretation of what God is doing, even an interpretation we think we have derived from the sacred scriptures, with God's design itself, we are underestimating God's plan and measuring God's wisdom by our own.

Yet the law of human intelligence is to search for a unifying principle. It is my conclusion that if we seek that unifying principle in any text or series of texts from the Bible the unification will be a constriction which artificially narrows the scope of God's action and locks us into one portion of God's revelation shut off from the rest. As we argued at the end of Chapter Three, the unifying principle of Christian faith and life is not an idea or an ideology and we might add, not a text even an inspired one. It is a person, Jesus himself, greater than any words (even when inspired) can capture, and the living community which is his body and his continuing presence. There has been an understandable reluctance on the part of Protestants to accept the community as the unifying principle of Christian faith because they are reluctant to accept a source of guidance which stands outside and independent of the Bible, rather than under the judgement of God's word, but the growing understanding in our day that the church is not outside the Bible nor the Bible outside the church but that both stand inseparably inside each other, the church interpreting and drawing life from the Bible and the Bible keeping the church faithful to its original mission, augurs well for the possibility of wider ecumenical agreement.

There is one further species of sectarianism in the use of the Bible that I want to examine before leaving this first example of the practical demands of catholicity. Up to the present the sectarian approaches to the Bible which we have considered are those which appeal to ordinary believers, but it is biblical specialists who are most tempted by this last form of narrowness.

The application of critical historical method to the biblical books is of quite recent date. The statement may seem exaggerated in the light of the very profound study of sacred scripture with which the fathers of the church and later theologians filled libraries. Much of this work is truly historical because in the last analysis history is what Christianity is all about, and no serious Christian can be unconcerned about facts especially when they impinge upon the one event on which the whole structure of faith depends. Still there is enough distinctive about the methodology developed by nineteenth century historiographers to say that it constitutes a new scientific discipline. What characterizes this methodology is its search for the bare facts—what exactly was done and said in what concrete historical circumstances. Ideally it excludes all presuppositions and all judgements of faith, because it is seeking to establish the unadorned factual basis on which interpretations must be based. In actuality no such totally neutral and sheerly factual record is ever achieved; presuppositions are always present even if they go unrecognized, but the effort to follow such a methodology did create a new form of scientific history which differs significantly from the faith filled efforts to understand and explain the sacred scripture found in the fathers of the church and from later commentaries and polemical works which ambition no such complete separation between the literal interpretation of the text and the theological judgement of the commentator.

At first the application of this new kind of literary and scientific-historical criticism to the Bible was resisted by the Christian churches, as it still is in some circles, but in general most educated Christians have come to accept that it has a perfectly legitimate though limited role to play in understanding the Bible. The new historical methodology does not imply that its practioner is an unbeliever; rather its validity rests on the intellectual power to prescind, to focus on one aspect of a complex reality at a time with no implication that what is discovered from that angle of vision is all there is to be discovered. It enables us to separate what we know from one source from what we know from others, making an accurate understanding of a text and dialogue about it much easier.

There has grown up a large body of exegetical studies of tremendous value to anyone who treasures the Bible, studies which make possible a fresh grasp of what the inspired author intended to say as distinguished from what later interpretation, often with perfect legitimacy, has added. One consequence has been a degree of ecumenical progress which could never have happened without this new biblical scholarship, a progress dramatically illustrated by the joint studies produced by theologians of different Christian traditions on subjects of controversy between them.[5] As long as theologians of different traditions attributed precisions and developments deriving from the faith filled and Spirit guided experience of a later generation to the plain and literal text of the Bible, misunderstanding was assured. But as theologians of all traditions came to appreciate more the gradual historical development of the Biblical text itself and to learn from advances in the new science of hermeneutics that the meaning of a text is never simple nor static, old entrenched positions could be abandoned and new agreement became possible.

Yet the proliferation of scientific biblical studies has not been an unmixed blessing. Biblical scholars never suggested that the results of their own research, done within the limits of their own restricted methodology, were all that the Bible could offer nor even its most important fruits. Their interest is so great, however, and the process of scientific biblical study so fascinating that this way of dealing with the sacred scriptures tends to get a preponderant or even an exclusive place in our use of the Bible. Precision does not imply exclusion of other aspects of the reality concerned but in practice it tends to take full possession of the field, and this imperialistic temptation has threatened not only biblical scholars themselves but most others who have become aware of their work. The result is impoverishing to the spirituality and theological wisdom of contemporary Christians. Reading a biblical passage can become a lesson in historical criticism rather than a contact with the living God in the community where he is still at work.

Two factors can serve as a corrective, protecting the Bible against any undue restriction within the limits of a neutral scientific methodology; one is secular and recent, the other lodged in a very ancient Christian tradition. First the secular. The pendulum has swung in textural studies (biblical and other) away from a narrow concentration on the text itself in its original historical setting to the larger question of meaning (hermeneutics). Why should anyone be interested in any ancient text? Some people no doubt are simply curious, but this is antiquarian interest and hardly widespread and it does not really deserve the name of history. It certainly does not correspond to the interest believers have in the sacred writings. If people read, ponder and pray an ancient text, it is because it has something to say to them now. Its meaning is not locked into a past experience of people long since dead. The process of discovering the meaning of any text—if it is at all profound—is not static, it is never complete. Each new generation can see more in the text than its predecessors and may also miss some aspects which its predecessors saw. Meaning is a relationship between a text and a reader or hearer, or a community of readers and hearers. Since the latter is always changing the meaning is never fixed and final.

When the people of Israel read the story of God's original deliverance of his people from Egypt, after they had experienced a new and different deliverance from the Babylonian exile, they saw more meaning there than the people who experienced the first exodus. When St. Stephan retold the story of Israel's history in the seventh chapter of the *Acts of the Apostles,* he did so in the light of the crucifixion and resurrection of Jesus, recognizing depths of meaning in the earlier events which could never have been discerned before. When Christians of the second and third centuries reflected on Jesus' words at the feast of Booths in Jerusalem, they found depths of meaning there which the original hearers would necessarily have missed.[6]

Is this to suggest that meanings are "read into" earlier words and events, that meaning is purely subjective? Certainly not. Rather the potentialities of any great word or event are unlimited. The meaning is truly there in the words and events but as a potentiality which only the unfolding of history will make clear. Meanings discovered later are not free floating; they must be solidly grounded in that initial word and event, but only later experience and reflection will permit them to emerge. A notable feature of every literary classic is that it can be read again and again, each time divulging more meaning than the last. If this is true of any classic, it is supremely true of a book which has God for its author and whose purpose is to record what the infinite and eternal God has done and is doing in our world.

This last observation leads us to the second corrective referred to above. It takes us back to the early Christian centuries but fits well with contemporary hermeneutics. The fathers of the church recognized that there was more than one meaning to the sacred scripture. By the early Middle Ages it had become customary to distinguish four senses: one, the literal meaning of the text, closest to what we described above as the meaning sought by modern exegetes; second, an analogical or mystical or spiritual meaning, because what is said literally may suggest by way of symbol, analogy or metaphor other realities than those directly referred to; third, a tropological sense, which drew out the implications for conduct in a biblical text, uncovering what guidance the ancient text offers us here and now for the living out of our Christian vocation; and finally a typical or anagogical sense, to which we shall return shortly.[7] Terminology differs and divisions overlap, but what is significant is the recognition that the meaning of a scriptural text goes far beyond the literal meaning intended by the original author. To conclude that a biblical author did not intend or even could not have intended a particular meaning does not prove that the biblical text does not have that meaning objectively. This may seem a strange assertion but it is testimony to the belief that God had an altogether singular role in the composition of this book. If the human author was an instrument in the hands of God, it is not unreasonable to suppose that he himself did not see beyond the immediate point he was making, but that the Holy Spirit, who was using him as an instrument did. Even in works where there is no question of divine inspiration, it is not uncommon for an author to see only imperfectly the implications of his own insights. How much more might not this be the case in the Bible, if it is truly God's book?

The last of the senses mentioned above—the typical sense—has special pertinence here. It was the conviction of the fathers of the church that not just the words of the sacred writings but the events and realities those words describe can point beyond themselves to persons and events in the future, which is what was meant by calling them "types." The supposition is that one great plan is at work in the world. Earlier events prepare for later ones. Those experiencing and writing about the earlier events are unaware of what lies ahead on the road they are traveling, but God knows how they fit into his plan thus the reference to the fulfillment to come is real and objective. It is rooted in the things and events described rather than simply in the mind of the author. From this perspective Christian tradition has spoken of a typical sense in the sacred scriptures, seeing, for example, language about the paschal lamb used for sacrifice in the Old Testament as in a deeper and more spiritual sense a symbol and foreshadowing of the One whose sacrifice on Calvary accomplishes supereminently what the older sacrifices were trying imperfectly to do (the "Lamb of God") and in the deliverance of the chosen people from their slavery in Egypt, a type or anticipation of the deliverance of all humanity by Jesus Christ from the slavery of sin and death into the promised land of eternal life.

The subject of the many senses of scripture can only be suggested here; it deserves a book in itself. I shall be satisfied if what has been said here demonstrates that it would be unacceptable to limit the meaning of the sacred scriptures to what can be determined by the use of neutral, scientific-historical methods of exegesis, as the best exegetes have always known and are saying increasingly at present. Even in secular terms such a limitation would be a human impoverishment, but in the case of believers it would cut them off from the best nourishment the Bible can offer their faith and spirituality. A catholic approach to the sacred writings is to look *at* them, indeed, using all the resources presently available for understanding, but also to look *through* them to what no purely rational or humanistic techniques can discern. If they are read in faith, they are a contact here and now with the Holy Spirit and a word of guidance for our own lives, not a historical curiosity about the distant past. As we have insisted so often before, catholicity requires openness. Faced with the voluminous results of modern critical scholarship dealing with the Bible, Christians are tempted either to jettison the spiritual riches nineteen centuries of Christian prayer and reflection have bequeathed to them or to reject blindly the whole project of such historical scholarship. Either alternative is disastrous. More than ever before the catholic policy of bringing the two together, not simplistically but with critical intelligence, is the only satisfactory answer. Finally, it seems evident that such a task is beyond the resources of any individual, however learned, and points up again the communitarian character imperative for Christian life in our day.

Open to Creation

We have been looking for examples of openness, that openness which is the essential requirement for being catholic. Openness to give and to receive. The example I want to explore in this section is the largest openness of all, large enough to be vague and ambiguous but specific instances may give it more definite shape. Let us call it openness to the world. The church is situated in an environment; how does or should she relate to that environment? One possible stance is defensive and hostile. She can be satisfied with her own resources, eager to share them with outsiders but suspicious of what is outside and unwilling to be changed herself in the process of changing others. It is the familiar sectarian mentality. Are there grounds for a more positive approach? They are to be found in the Christian dogma of creation.

According to Christian faith God is related to the world in two ways, connected but distinct. Everything that is owes its total being to God. It could not begin to be nor continue to be and to act except for the real and present gift coming from God. Over and above this initial and completely universal relationship, God has involved himself in a new and personal way in the affairs of humanity. Within this world created by God there has been and continues to be a series of particular events leading up to and culminating in the life, death and resurrection of Jesus Christ and extending Jesus' mission until he comes again. God relates to the world, then, not only as its creator but also as its redeemer. Clearly this latter relationship receives preponderant attention in the sacred scriptures and in the teaching, life and prayer of the church, but the doctrine of creation, though not as exalted as that of redemption, also belongs unquestionably to the essence of Christian faith. The liturgy of the Easter Vigil is right in asking, "What good would life have been to us, had Christ not come as our Redeemer?" but all that is ours by birth into the human family and all that the world includes simply because it exists—all this, too, is a gift of God. The greater gifts of redemption, moreover, flow back over this first bounty of God, giving it a much greater dignity than it could have had by itself but depending on it, too, as the flower depends on the earth where it is planted, or to use a metaphor which does more justice to the internal connection between these two dogmas of faith, the redemptive grace of Jesus is plunged into the center of creation, permeating and transforming the whole and pointing it in a new direction. Creation does more than provide a stage on which the great redemptive acts are played out. There is only one plan of God, which comes to fruition in Jesus, his Son. Both creation and redemption are part of this one plan and there is no way of separating them into independent units. The whole of creation is marked internally, therefore, by God's gift of his own Son as redeemer of the world.

The dogma of creation is the *magna charta* of a catholic view of the world. I suggest that a sectarian approach to the world outside the church is insufficiently attentive to the Christian doctrine of creation and too exclusively preoccupied with redemption, whereas catholicity is open to both articles of faith: creation and redemption.

The implications of believing in creation are far-reaching. It means that anything humanity discovers, even if it has no explicit relation to faith, is light from God and must be respected and treasured. Human intelligence and sensibility are friends and allies of God's grace and never to be despised. It means that the evils in our world can never be blamed on art, science and technology in themselves, although all can be put to evil use. It requires respect for every culture, however untouched it may seem by the gospel, because wherever men and women have tried to understand, use and appreciate the world around them, they have been in contact with God. Literature, scientific progress, the search for better ways to organize society and for more efficient use of material resources, joy in human companionship and in all the good things the earth has to offer: these things are not distractions from the service of God but holy in themselves even before any blessing has been said over them. There is a certain radical optimism inseparable from the dogma of creation. It is wrong to turn our backs on the good things God has given us, wrong to prefer the spiritual riches of Christian faith in such a way that the good things of nature are downgraded.

Yet the picture we have just painted is obviously over-simplified and needs correction. The world which God created does not come to us in idyllic form. Often enough it is only as marked by greed and cruelty that we contact it. Science and technology far from being an invitation to serve God often present themselves as instruments for exploitation; art and entertainment can corrupt as well as nourish us. To believe in creation is not to look at the world through the eyes of Pollyanna. Christian faith is fully aware of the fact of sin, not as an occasional deviation which mars the surface but as a powerful force deep in the fabric of humanity and therefore permeating and deforming the material world in so far as sinful human beings extend their mastery over it. There is nothing arbitrary about the doctrine of the cross. In a world where sin has made deep inroads, discovering and responding to God's purpose and the signs of his presence in creation call for self-denial and sacrifice.

We have here another of those dichotomies which call for a catholic or integrating response, clinging to both poles of the tension and refusing to exaggerate either. There is an abundance of sin and evil in the world God created; renunciation and self sacrifice, therefore, are an inescapable demand for Christian living, but the underlying worth of everything God has made is not effaced by human sinfulness, hence Christians can never surrender the world or anything in it to the power of Satan. All is redeemable, because it is first and always linked to God by creation. The Christian holds a double citizenship, one by reason of human birth and the other by birth of water and the Holy Spirit, and while the two allegiances overlap, the rights and duties proper to each are not identical. Being faithful to both allegiances is more difficult than choosing one and forgetting about the other. However heroic it may seem to turn one's back on the world and devote oneself exclusively to those activities obviously and explicitly linked to God, this can be a way of escaping rather than embracing the cross, for anyone who tries to bring together the world and the gospel will experience opposition, ridicule and a large measure of short range failure.

How in practical terms a Christian responds to the essential goodness of creation within a world marred by sin is too large a question to be taken up here. I introduce it only to guard against a naive and over simplified notion of the openness to the world called for by catholicity. An openness which is easy and comfortable is certainly a betrayal of Christian faith. For example one who believes in the dogma of creation will approach scientific research with a positive attitude. He will be eager to listen and to learn, to appropriate new insights and new techniques. He will be open to the criticism such scientific work brings to bear on traditional theories and practices. However, he will not swallow whole everything which is advanced in the name of scientific progress. Christian faith is not an empty form which can be filled with any content. It is not a vague sentiment which can adopt any contemporary fad, even if it claims the title of the latest advance in science or psychology. The gospel does not consist of bland platitudes; it has a bite that challenges and confronts what passes for wisdom in the world. The Christian faith is not an aura of sentimentality that can surround anything it meets; it has solid and objective content. The tradition of the Christian church is based on centuries of experience and reflection, guided by the Holy Spirit. So Christian faith does not come as a mute and passive partner to its conversation with the world, it has very definite things to say about God, man and the world. Openness requires dialogue but there is no dialogue when only one side is speaking.

Perhaps this needs emphasis today. I think it is fair to say that many Christians, especially Catholic Christians, have become unduly apologetic. The defensiveness which characterized Christians in the nineteenth century has quite suddenly been succeeded by a desire to catch up with the times and to adapt to all those developments in the modern world, which until quite recently were regarded with suspicion and hostility. There is danger of uncritical enthusiasm for trends which, though once extremely popular, have most recently come under attack from secular thinkers for reasons remarkably similar to those advanced by traditional Catholic sources. In too many cases, for example, religious education and programs in spirituality were exchanged for psychological self help sessions patterned after the latest theories in psychology and group dynamics. There is no question but what Christians have much to learn from developments in these fields but the kind of openness envisioned here does not call for believers to come empty handed to the dialogue. They must ask whether the presuppositions brought to these workshops conflict with the vision of life that comes to us through Jesus Christ. Do they presume an exclusive orientation on this life? Do they allow room for sacrifice and the doctrine of the cross? Is their image of happiness and fulfillment consistent with the gospel? I am not suggesting a negative answer to these questions but a truly Christian openness requires that the questions be asked. Again believers should be eager to profit from more efficient management and communication technique but they must ask what measure is being used to judge efficiency. How does it relate to the image of life given us by our faith? Democratic decision making and newly perfected sociological methods for determining grass roots sentiment belong within the Christian community but it would be wrong to think they can substitute for the Holy Spirit and the substance of tradition.

What has been said just above is offered simply as a caution against a soft and over-simplified receptivity to the world, but let us return to the main line of argument by spelling out in more detail what this receptivity should involve. For many Christians faith and reason are treated as antonyms; to choose faith is to leave reason behind; to look for rational grounds for believing in God or in what God has revealed betrays a lack of faith. With the Roman Catholic tradition, I suggest that no such opposition is justified. There is nothing wrong with seeking answers to the great human questions with all the resources available to our humanity as long as is done with that humility which not only the gospel but also the great humanistic philosophers demand. Human reason will never substitute for faith but it can facilitate and support it. Thus there should be genuine sympathy for what all great thinkers, ancient and modern, believers and unbelievers, have contributed to the wisdom of mankind. It is no accident that the modern university has its origin in the Christian church. Thomas Aquinas was carrying on the same great tradition of openness when he made the philosophy of Aristotle, which came to him by way of Islamic thinkers, the framework for synthesizing Christian theology, and more recently the same universalistic instinct has led Christian thinkers to welcome the insights of existentialism, phenomenology and process thought and the social analyses of Marxism for the enrichment of a Christian vision of the world. None of these secular sources can be accepted simply as such, of course; they must be sifted through the sieve of Christian faith and no true Christian doubts which side must yield in cases of conflict, but out of the process comes a more catholic Christianity.

Perhaps at the present time the most widely discussed example of openness goes by the name of inculturation. When the community composed of those already baptized begins to penetrate civilizations previously remote, what approach will she take to the culture of her converts and those who, even if never converted, enter into a new conversation with Christianity? The universal human tendency is to package together all of the constituents of our culture, thereby mingling and confusing those deriving from Christian faith with those peculiar to our own place and people and identifying the whole as the content of Christian faith and life to be transmitted to others. Too often Christians have yielded to this common tendency but it is also true that from the beginning a counter trend has been at work, which testifies to the essential catholicity belonging to the church of Christ. The language and symbols, the music, art and customs of the newcomers have been welcomed and assimilated to produce new cultures where Christianity has become incarnate in a different way. The Greco-Roman world of the first few centuries, the Byzantine civilization of eastern Europe, and western Europe of the Middle Ages are notable examples. Our forefathers did not hesitate to pattern their ecclesial institutions on Roman models nor to transform customs and symbols of the Germanic tribes into Christian forms, anymore than our Old Testament forebears hesitated to adapt the songs and stories of their pagan Semitic neighbors for the honor and service of Yahweh. To some, such borrowing has been scandalous, but in fact it is testimony to the unity of God's plan for the whole human family and the dynamism he has instilled into his people to reach out beyond themselves toward all mankind.

If this book were a history of what Christians have actually done in their dealings with other cultures, in contrast to what they should have done, it would be easy to draw up a painful indictment of blindness and cultural imperialism. Churches built in Gothic style architecture in the middle of India, Latin liturgical language imposed on Japanese converts, European patterns of behavior confused with universal moral norms and prescribed in circumstances where they were arbitrary and out of place: all such things are proof that we have a long way to go to achieve the ideal of catholicity. But our purpose is not to write a history of catholicity as practiced (or neglected) in the past but a prescription for the present, and those many failures should not obscure the fact that assimilation has occurred, slowly and falteringly to be sure, but undeniably, and today there is an unprecedented determination to respect and learn from other cultures.

What has been said so far has general application to the whole course of Christian history. It is always necessary for the church to be interested in and receptive to things non-Christian and to avoid any form of insularity, but at present there is an altogether special urgency for the church to resist self-enclosure or preoccupation with her own internal concerns. Only by involving herself with secular issues, by joining in the debates going on in the marketplace, the legislative assembly and the nonsectarian university can the church fulfill even her own internal responsibilities. Confinement within the so-called "religious" sphere has never been more disastrous for Christians than in our day. Let me propose three reasons why this is true. First, there is the simple fact of greatly increased communication. There are scarcely any secluded enclaves in our civilization, except perhaps where authoritarian governments have succeeded in imposing strict controls and even these controls are by no means fully effective. Almost everyone is in touch with the great religious and cultural pluralism of our world. The days when the family could defend a privileged and protected role in passing on its cultural heritage to its children are past, and what is said of the family applies with greater force to less fundamental social units like the school and the parish. Behind much current criticism of the failure of schools to transmit moral and religious values lies a greatly exaggerated estimate of the place schools occupy among the influences affecting students in a society as open as ours. This means that if parents or religious groups think they can safeguard the faith and morals of their children by keeping out alien influences, they are sadly mistaken. There are no barriers thick enough to exclude the diverse voices in the world around us. Our very pluralistic culture is as close as the nearest television set or newspaper stand. This is not to argue against every attempt at parental or wider societal guidance but it is to acknowledge that such efforts by themselves will always be inadequate. If Christians today live a Christian life, it will not be because they have never encountered different images of life. The corporate responsibility of the Christian community is not to exclude other influences—a hopeless task in any case—but to help all its members develop a mature faith which can cope intelligently with the many sided diversity of our society and a freely chosen self-dicipline, based not on ignorance of other options but on informed choice.

Secondly, there is the fact of secularization. Many have had second thoughts about just how extensive the process of secularization is in the modern world, nonetheless it seems evident, at least in western civilization, that the process of dealing with the ordinary business of life without introducing properly religious or explicitly Christian considerations has been proceeding apace. Religious symbols are often invoked but their place is marginal. The substance of human life, family relations, education, political and economic decisions are increasingly governed by neutral considerations, owing little but rhetoric to Christian faith. The vision of life we discover in movies, plays, soap operas and popular songs betrays only the most superficial relation to Christian faith. For everyone who seeks moral and spiritual guidance from priest, minister or rabbi, there are probably several who turn to Ann Landers or Joyce Brothers. What has this to do with catholicity? Simply this: if Christianity is to meet modern people, it has to meet them where they are and the secular is where they are.

There is a further consideration, somewhat more subtle but probably more significant. The religious instinct is deep and widespread even in our secular age. If the Christian church were willing to devote her energies almost exclusively to satisfying the religious instinct by providing occasions for prayer, ritual and human companionship in a religious setting, she would perform a much appreciated service, but she would betray her vocation to walk in the footsteps of Jesus. This would be the religion of the Pharisees rather than that of Jesus. It is hard to think of anything more alien to Jesus (and to the Old Testament prophets as well) than a religion centered on ceremonial and leaving untouched the substance of human activities. She would be conforming as well to the distorted image of religion proposed by Feuerbach, Nietzsche and Marx as an alienating force in human life, distracting people from the serious business of living by ersatz satisfactions. To use the language of an earlier chapter, if the church were to concentrate on strictly "religious" or sacred activities, she could gain in horizontal catholicity but she would lose much in vertical catholicity. She would have a wide popular appeal because her demands would be confined to a very limited segment of life and her awards would be attractive if ephemeral, but she would be touching only a shallow segment of human existence. There might be more Christians but there would be little Christian life. In our secularized civilization, more than ever before, if Christianity is to leaven humanity, to convert and transform people to the roots of their existence, rather than to gild the externals with religious decoration, it must come to grips with the world and the secular activities where most of life is lived.

Finally, there is the unprecedented encounter between Christianity and other world religions in our time. If there is to be a dialogue between Christianity and the great Asian religions, for example, it cannot take place on the level of a shared biblical tradition. Christians believe that the effects of the one redemption brought about by Jesus on Calvary extend to all mankind. They cannot, then, be confined within the limits of the explicit preaching of the gospel. The logic of faith compels us to acknowledge that in relating to the non-Christian world, we are not dealing with something "purely natural." The supernatural grace of God in Jesus Christ has been and is at work within this world where the visible agencies of the church have not reached, and if we want to respond to the universal dimension of the Christian vocation, we must be receptive to God's action and revelation within the secular or at least non-Christian world. It needs to be remembered as well that if we understand the term *religion* in the wide sense it is frequently given in academic circles today, as any system of beliefs or assumptions, whereby men and women try to make sense of and deal with the whole of reality, rather than just the pragmatic concerns of everyday living, then one of the most widespread of world religions of our times is secular humanism. In spite of its non-religious appearance, it is secular humanism which for great numbers of people on all continents, performs the function more traditional religions used to (and still do) perform for others. If the mission of the Christian church is universal, then she urgently needs to dialogue today with secular humanism and for this dialogue she must be open to the secular world.

It may be helpful at this point to recall the main line of argument in this chapter lest we get lost in details. Having argued in general terms that the church of Christ must be catholic, we are exploring three major examples of what catholicity means in practice. To be catholic, the church must be open to all of her own resources, never confining her interest to any part of them to the exclusion of the rest, and our first example was that great primary resource which is the Bible. The church must be open to the whole of the Bible in all of its dimensions. Shortly we will turn our attention to the need for openness to the rest of her own resources other than the Bible, but for the present we are exploring the demand catholicity imposes to be open to resources which are not her own, to the world beyond her borders, that world which relates to God because he created all of it, but which has not been gathered into the Christian church and marked, at least consciously and externally, by the historical mission of Jesus and his church. Let me put it another way. What is at issue here is the church's relationship to the non-Christian world and especially to its most important segment: the secular sphere of human life, that immense arena of human activity which is neutral to and independent of the Christian (or any other) religion. I have been arguing that a church which addressed itself exclusively to "religion" would be singularly ineffectual in our highly secular age.

Before leaving this topic I want to suggest how the church can come to grips with the secular in practice, lest what we are saying remain too theoretical. There are two movements which illustrate how the church of Christ can achieve presence within the secular domain. I offer them only as examples which could be multiplied many times over. The first is the Young Christian Workers movement (YCW or in French, JOC, *Jeunesse Ouvrière Chrétienne*), pioneered by a young Belgian priest, Joseph Cardign (later Cardinal) in the early decades of this century. Cardign developed a pattern for the meetings of these young committed believers, themselves actively engaged in the very secular atmosphere of shop and factory, which has exerted great influence on Christian apostolic ministry in the twentieth century. The pattern can be summarized in three words: observe, judge and act. We must observe and study and be intelligently aware of the environment in which our lives are lived, then we must judge or evaluate this environment in the light of a deep, prayerful study of the gospel and finally we must act together to bring the light of the gospel into that environment where not only our own but countless other lives are lived.

My other example is the phenomenal growth of Basic Christian Communities, mostly in Latin America but also in Europe and elsewhere. These communities are very much a part of the secular world, though it is their faith in Jesus which brings them together, and motivates and directs them in their task of responding to the full human needs of their own members and of the societies of which they form part.

In both cases it is lay people who provide not only the rank and file but also a large part of the leadership of the community, which is itself a protection against preoccupation with internal, ecclesiastical goals. In both cases, too, the apostolic action of the group is directed not simply to worship, prayer and other "religious" activities but to all areas of life: familial, economic, social, educational, etc. The gospel is seen as a leaven, intended to penetrate and transform the secular world.

There is one other aspect of Christian openness to the world which must be taken up before we leave this subject. It is related to what we have just been saying about the secularization of modern life but sufficiently distinct to deserve special attention and so overwhelmingly important that it would be wrong to omit it. I have in mind an openness to the world, which weighs upon the conscience of Christians not simply because it is needed to be relevant nor even because it is a logical corollary of Christian faith. The international synod of Roman Catholic Bishops meeting in Rome in 1971 stated it clearly in their final document.

> Action on behalf of justice and participation in the transformation of the world clearly appear to us as an essential dimension of the preaching of the Gospel—or in other words, of the Church's mission for the redemption of the human race and its liberation from every oppressive situation.[8]

The mission of Jesus, as it is made known in the Gospels, does not consist in getting people into Heaven after they die. The message of the gospel is addressed to people here and now in the very concrete circumstances of the present. It is indeed a promise of eternal life, but not an eternal life which begins when we die, but now, in the flesh and blood reality of this world. The test of whether we shall possess that eternal kingdom, according to Jesus' description of the final judgement, is how we have responded to the needs of our brothers and sisters in this world—and it is surely significant that the needs singled out are all material, e.g., food, drink.[9] The rest of the New Testament reiterates and specifies this central obligation of Christian living to meet each other's temporal needs.

What the synod affirmed, then, is thoroughly in keeping with the New Testament. In the face of injustice and suffering of such magnitude in the world around us, the search for better and more just conditions is not simply consistent with or encouraged by the gospel; it *is* the gospel, an intrinsic constituent of it ("essential dimension"). If there is one conviction that has been growing among Christians of all denominations and tendencies, at least in the person of their official representatives, it is that Christians must involve themselves more with the secular problems of our age: international relations, nuclear disarmament, world hunger, defense of human rights, a more just distribution of this world's goods. Dietrich Bonhoeffer, the great Lutheran pastor and theologian, who was martyred for his opposition to Hitler, is a symbol and prophet of this ecumenical trend and his call for a Christianity deeply engaged in the great secular problems of our age, and spurning the comfort of an individualistic and pietistical form of religion, has resounded widely in the minds and hearts of contemporary Christians.

Involvement can take many forms and it is no part of our purpose here to discuss how Christians and Christian organizations should go about their involvement in the secular problems of our age. For our present purpose it is sufficient to point out that it demands an unprecedented openness to the world. Today more than ever a purely "spiritual" religion would betray the Christian vocation. For Christians to be bottled up within their own communities, interested only in their own religious development, and occupied exclusively with their intramural problems, when the human needs of the world around are so great and the threats to human survival so fearsome, is not simply unwise, it is in contradiction to the very essence of their faith.

Let no one think that this call to reach out to our neighbor in need is answered by individual acts of compassion. Now as always such individual acts are necessary and important; furthermore they are close at hand and relatively simple, but in our highly complex society, where decisions of government, corporation or labor union have more effect on the happiness (or misery) of millions than hundreds of charity drives, they are insufficient. Minimally we can say that unless attention is directed to the underlying causes of injustice—political, economic, social—as well as to assisting individual victims of unjust social systems, the results will be meager indeed.

One last observation is appropriate. It is clear that the kind of openness to the world which is needed for the church to be catholic is far beyond the means of any individual. No one could hope to master more than a fragment of the information required or to possess more than a few of the necessary skills. Only a community can measure up to the demands of Christian faith. An individualistic Christian faith and life is utterly inadequate to the demands of the Christian vocation in our day.

Revelation Comes in Many Ways

There is one more example of openness or catholicity which I want to explore in this chapter. Let me introduce it by calling attention to the problem it alone can solve. Christians are presently experiencing great confusion touching on what they believe and how they should live. The confusion is general but let us focus for the moment on the most fundamental of all questions of faith: Jesus himself—who is he? Within the last few decades books on Jesus have proliferated as have plays, movies, periodical articles and talk shows on radio and television. How different the answers offered to this question on which the whole of Christian faith depends! In some cases the credentials of the author or the sensational nature of the presentation make it evident that what is said cannot be taken seriously, but even in such cases it is not easy for the ordinary believer to distinguish responsible scholarship from flimsy imitations. But also among authors who are unquestionably sincere and whose scholarly credentials are impeccable, vastly divergent images of Jesus appear.

Now there is a diversity of understanding which is simply the mark of richness and depth in the reality to be understood. This kind of diversity in the image of Jesus is found in the Gospels and in all the tradition of the church, but the diversity at issue here is much more radical. It is a diversity of contradiction rather than of complementarity. Jesus, as imaged in many modern studies has little in common with Jesus as worshipped and followed by centuries of Christians; he bears little resemblance to the Only Begotten Son of God described by the Council of Chalcedon and the other early councils of the church; he is in no recognizable sense the founder of Christianity as it has developed historically over the centuries. Certainly this is not to suggest that those scholars who have tried to understand Jesus afresh and to express their understanding in language meaningful to their contemporaries are uniformly heretical. Nor is it to suggest that orthodoxy is best served by those who are content to repeat traditional formulas of faith in language which has become unintelligible if not positively misleading to educated people of our time. However, even authentically

Christian studies are remarkably diverse in their interpretations and contribute to the confusion experienced by believers.

We ought not be surprised that people in our day give such varied answers to the question, "Who is Jesus?," when at Caeserea Philippi, Jesus himself received very different answers to the same question, and when Simon Peter proclaimed the answer of orthodox faith, Jesus attributed his discovery not to intelligence or to historical scholarship but to the Father's revelation.[10] So the first word that needs to be said about learning the identity of Jesus is that only the supernatural grace of God can make it known, but this is not the last word, since the question still remains how and where in the midst of all the confusion and diversity even among sincere believers desiring to be guided by the Holy Spirit, God's revelation is to be found. This is where our final example of openness is pertinent.

But before we discuss it, let us avert to another major area of confusion, which is even more disturbing to believers because it touches their lives so directly. I am thinking about the widespread dissention on moral questions. Traditional norms about marriage, family life, premarital sex, homosexuality, etc. have been called into question on all sides. There is nothing new about varying practice in matters of morality but today the norms themselves, once almost universally accepted in our western civilization, are under attack to an unprecedented degree. Nor can it be maintained that those who make this challenge are uninformed or immoral people. Sincere and respected Christian thinkers can be found on different sides of the debated questions. It is no part of our purpose here to offer answers to the disputed questions; our sole concern is the way of answering. Where do you look for your answer?

What is called for, I suggest, is openness to *all* the sources of God's revelation. Many of our problems in doctrinal and moral questions come from exclusive or excessive concentration on one avenue by which God approaches us. It is important not to block off any of the channels which connect us with God.

Let me enumerate some of them. First of all the sacred scriptures, in all their breadth and variety. We have seen already how many-sided this source of God's communication is, and we have insisted that fidelity to the inspired word of God demands that the whole of the Bible in all its multiplicity be embraced. But the utterly divergent images of Jesus that come to us from highly qualified and completely sincere students of the New Testament testify dramatically that the Bible is not enough. If skilled, sensitive and prayerful scholars can come up with such contradictory conclusions, then the Bible by itself is not enough.

What we are doing in fact, if on principle we limit God's revelation to the Bible alone, is to deliver ourselves over to our favorite biblical experts. Interpreting the Bible with the help of the literary and historical techniques available at present is a task that demands years of preparation. Relatively few have time and talent to undertake it. Even among those who do, the whole Bible is too large a field for expertise; specialization in some part is necessary for genuine mastery, which is one of the reasons for the great diversity we mentioned earlier, for a scholar will inevitably give more weight to certain books or aspects than to others; the limits of intelligence and sensitivity require it. One weakness, for example, in many of the new studies of Jesus is that they concentrate predominantly if not exclusively on some New Testament books, especially the synoptic gospels and dismiss evidence from the gospel of John and the later New Testament authors. If, however, one accepts the whole New Testament as a Spirit-guided interpretation of Jesus, then such exclusivity can only give an unbalanced picture.

If the Bible is truly a human document (as it surely is, though faith assures us that it is also much more) which requires interpretation by all the skills available, then we are dependent on experts and the end result is that what passes for faith in the sacred scriptures is more immediately faith in the particular experts whose interpretation we choose to follow (and faith it is which is involved, because we have neither time nor resources sufficient for an independent evaluation). Such faith is more demanding and enjoys less guarantees than the faith usually asked of Christians.

What connects us with God is not just a book, even a sacred one. Jesus Christ is not a first century hero whose memory and teaching guide us today through the written record which has been preserved. He is risen and alive, not separated from us by a gap of nineteen centuries. So the written word is not the only source of God's communication. The Eucharist, the other Sacraments and the liturgy and prayer of the church are channels of communication with God. They do not deliver a new message, independent of the sacred scriptures, because written word and sacramental action are always inseparably mingled in the church's practice, but on the other hand they are not simply an external support to a message fully contained in the Bible. They are an intrinsic part of the message. The notion that the text of the Bible is the sole source of our knowledge of God's revelation rests upon an outdated understanding of the place of verbal expression within the much wider reality of communication. When persons encounter each other, the written or spoken words which pass between them are by no means the whole of their self-disclosure to each other. Since the invention of printing we have been mesmerized by the written word, but under the influence of such thinkers as Marshall Mc-Luhan and Walter Ong, we are coming to a more modest but also more realistic evaluation of the place written words and formal language of any sort occupy within the much larger phenomenon of communication between persons.

The experience of the liturgy, which is an experience here and now of the risen Jesus and of his Spirit, is an integral part of the conversation between God and his people. Just how this experience supplies intellectual content to our dealings with God cannot be spelled out in rational terms, though I am sure the process could be analyzed in more detail than we shall attempt here. But then who could specify exactly how learning takes place in personal encounter, when only human persons are involved? When the Holy Spirit is among the participants a new element of mystery is introduced. The sacred scriptures will not deliver their full content in the classroom or library; when they are prayed and meditated while celebrating the Eucharist, new dimensions of their objective and internal reality will appear. To isolate the Bible from the Eucharist and the rest of the sacraments and prayer life of the church is to impoverish it. It is a temptation for academics to regard what can be learned through the use of their methods as the only objective, intellectual content, and to consign what remains to the domain of piety, emotion and subjectivism. In fact such a restriction is an unjustified narrowing of the evidence on which our judgements should be based.

Experience is always richer than any account of it. At the end of his gospel, St. John reflects that if all the things Jesus did were written down, there would scarcely be room enough in the whole world to contain the books necessary to record them.[11] Extending the principle beyond the personal history of Jesus himself to the experience of the whole community in which Jesus continues his life and mission, we can say that the experience of the church is incomparably larger than any books describing it. We might imagine the Bible as a handbook which guides Christians in living out their mission. As such the experience of living out the mission is the best commentary on the book, especially since Jesus has left us not just a book but his own Spirit to direct the process.

This suggests another avenue by which God makes himself known to his people: the experience of Christian living, not only the privileged experience of sacrament and prayer, but the total experience of those who have tried to live by the faith of Jesus. It is not simply that each of us can learn from our own experience, but the whole range of Christian history comes into play. Christians are not isolated individuals; they belong to a people and every bit of the experience of that people is theirs. In view of the covenant the history of that people from start to finish is lived in association with the Holy Spirit, which does not mean that it has always or even regularly been a story of docility to the Spirit, but whether by cooperating or resisting, all of it has been lived in interaction with the Holy Spirit within the special destiny given to the people of God and all of it can teach us about God. What Paul said about the experience of our Old Testament forebears can be extended to the whole story of the covenanted people, "The things that happened to them serve as an example. They have been written as a warning to us...".[12]

Among the great teachers of the Christian people, should certainly be numbered the saints, even or especially those who never wrote a book or stood in a pulpit. They have served as a kind of prism, focusing the light of the gospel, each in his or her own way on the particular situation in which their life was lived. Taken singly no one of them gives a full picture of Christian life and their appeal and educational usefulness are regularly limited by the peculiarities of their own time and temperament, but taken together they fill out very significantly the picture of life lived in the Spirit. They interpret the Christian message not by the methods of scientific exegesis but in the concrete reality of their lives as disciples of Jesus, with a kind of interpretation which is undoubtedly more effective than theoretical teaching. Mention ought to be made too, of the tradition and spiritual doctrine of the great religious orders, Benedictine, Carmelite, Dominican, Franciscan, Jesuit, etc. There is here a wealth of Christian wisdom, all of it pertinent to a full and balanced understanding of what Christianity is. Finally, though the list is by no means definitive, there are so many popular devotions which have waxed and waned over the course of the centuries. All are not equally central nor equally solid, but they carry with and in them a great deal of Christian experience, all of which is under the influence of the Holy Spirit.

It is popular devotions which translate the substance of faith into the vital, human experience of ordinary Christians. How many Christians have learned what they know of the Blessed Trinity, the Incarnation, the Redemption from the official creeds of the church, at least in a way which genuinely affects their lives? Anyone engaged in religious education has discovered that creeds and official formulations of faith can be recited thousands of times without ever taking root in the mind and heart of the one who recites them. The sacred scriptures have greater power to make contact with people where they are, because they are so much more concrete, but even there the Biblical narrative is sufficiently tied to the past and to unfamiliar ways of thinking that we can hear it read repeatedly without being deeply touched by what it is saying. I suggest that it is popular devotions which mediate the basic beliefs of Christian faith to most of the faithful more than any other source. Let me clarify what I mean here by "popular devotion." I am not thinking only of secondary and peripheral devotional practices such as special prayers to a patron saint, nor am I thinking of a new and independent source of God's action in our lives, over and above the basic sources, but of the whole complex of beliefs and practices—regularly built around Eucharist, Sacraments and Bible—which make up the religious experience of the Christian people at one time and place, some of it fundamental and some ephemeral, but all of it mingled in the mind, heart, memory, imagination and practice of believers. It is Christian experience as it has evolved over the centuries, and thus it includes much more than the original content of faith and the original structures of Christian life and prayer.

Popular devotion is not Christian faith in pure form, to be sure. In passing through the minds and hearts of people, all of whom are at best imperfect, it runs the risk of narrowing the content of God's revelation to what a particular group of believers finds appealing and worse of being contaminated by elements in the culture which do not derive from Jesus and may be thoroughly contrary to his Spirit, and so it must constantly be subjected to criticism in the light of the whole of God's word. Nonetheless, this darker side does not cancel out its positive role and certainly does not detract from its *de facto* importance in shaping the religious life of Christians.

Popular devotion derives from the more fundamental elements of faith, and it is necessarily connected with those fundamentals. The latter contention needs to be qualified but I believe it is true and important. A dogma of faith must produce cultural effects among the people who believe it: practices, celebrations, songs, sentiments, even myths and legends. Without them the dogmas would not be really and humanly believed. The form these cultural products of dogma take will vary with the culture; to that extent they are arbitrary, but not totally. There is a logic which connects them with the dogmas; that is to say, they are the expression in popular imagination and sentiment of what the dogmas demand. For example belief in eternal life necessarily results in concern for and interest in those who have died; there will be imagery, rituals, stories dealing with life beyond the grave. The imagery, etc. will differ with the culture involved and to that extent it is arbitrary but surely we could conclude that a culture which did not have any such practices or imagery does not really believe in eternal life.

A second conclusion follows from the linkage between popular devotion and the fundamental beliefs of faith. As essential Christian faith necessarily produces the development called popular devotion, so popular devotion determines what people really believe about the fundamentals of faith. If you eliminate a popular devotion you may be undermining the belief from which it sprang. A striking instance is at hand. From the earliest centuries great devotion sprang up in the Christian world to the Blessed Virgin Mary. This devotion rests upon the role of Mary witnessed to in the New Testament but it has expanded and developed greatly over the centuries especially in the eastern and Roman Catholic traditions. Think of all the churches and shrines, the feast days, hymns, prayers and practices honoring Mary, found all over the Christian world! It is the logic of the Incarnation which is responsible for this development. If people genuinely believe that Jesus of Nazareth is true God as well as true man, it is inevitable that they will reflect upon the one human being who was, by necessity, most uniquely related to him and on her continuing role in the kingdom of God. And since the logic in question is not simply one of the mind, but we might say, also a logic of the heart and of living human experience, it will issue in devotions, practices, prayers and sentiments. This is exactly what has happened over the course of Christian history.

It is true that devotion to Mary has been stimulated by the contingencies of history, for example, the struggle against Arianism in the fourth century led orthodox Christians to stress one-sidedly the divinity of Jesus and to underplay his humanity, and this in turn probably resulted in increased popular devotion to Mary as the one person closest to God while remaining exclusively and unequivocally on the side of human beings. The fact remains that devotion to Mary is a necessary consequence of vital, human belief in the Incarnation. If Jesus is truly the Son of God, sharing equally with the Father and the Holy Spirit in the one Divine Nature, then Mary's role in the plan of salvation becomes incomparably mysterious and will inescapably be the subject of prayer and reflection.

In recent decades belief in the divinity of Jesus has weakened among many Christians and the dogma of the Incarnation has been not so much denied as watered down and "demythologized." Isn't it interesting that at the same time devotion to Mary has been greatly reduced? It is hard not to see a connection between the two. To be sure the process is not formal and deliberate but it seems to me that the two developments affect each other. As concentration on the divine and supernatural in Jesus resulted quite naturally in an abundance of Marian devotion, so reducing Jesus to exclusively human dimensions (as much recent Christology has tended to do) has been accompanied by an abandonment of Marian devotion. Likewise as the great prevalence of Marian devotion in popular piety focussed the faith of ordinary Christians on Jesus as the Son of God, so its dramatic decline has weakened or deflected the ordinary believer's faith in Jesus as God Incarnate and has reinforced the tendency to see Jesus primarily as a prophet and a teacher and model of ethics.

What has occurred, it seems to me, is that many of the intellectual leaders in the churches have become more and more uncomfortable with the traditional understanding of the Incarnation as totally out of tune with the secular presuppositions of our age and this discomfort and embarrassment has naturally extended to Marian devotion. Since the discomfort has been felt more keenly among those in positions of leadership than among the rank and file, Marian devotion has been increasingly forgotten and neglected. The end result has been a further weakening of the traditional faith in the Incarnation among the Christian people in general. You cannot ignore the developments which have occurred over the centuries in the religious experience of believers without changing the originating faith, because these developments are (in part) the working out of the implications of that original faith. They are more than accidental accretions which can be brushed away to uncover the faith in its pristine form; they are bonds connecting us with that fundamental faith and translating it into the stuff of daily life. Damage to them will react upon their source.

The point we have been trying to make is that catholicity demands an openness and receptivity to all the works of grace during the centuries that separate us from the New Testament times. They must not be put on a par with the foundational events of the beginning, nor can we forget that the history of Christianity is always a mixture of God's grace with human weakness and sin, but it would be a great mistake to omit them from the picture, because they are concrete evidence of what God through Christ and in the Spirit has been doing in our world. Moreover, for one who believes in the resurrection and in the continuing presence of the Holy Spirit within the church, they are in a sense the Holy Spirit's own interpretation of the foundational events. A twentieth century understanding of Christianity based exclusively on first century documents is leaving out entirely too much.

Of course, none of us can know more than a small fraction of the heritage which is ours, but in the interaction of a vital community, where there are, in principle at least, no barriers blocking out any part of this immense heritage, we have grounds to hope that what is needed for our particular moment will be found.

We are left before a vast and multifaceted body of evidence through which God's revelation comes to us, vast not only in quantity but in kind. It is all pertinent and catholicity demands that none of it be discarded or isolated from the rest. Before such abundance the individual believer must feel like a child approaching the ocean with a little cup. But God does not deal with us as isolated individuals. Without diminishing in the least the immediate and personal relationship to each one, he gathers us together as a people, making us dependent on each other in order to be dependent on him. All of which leads to one more avenue of God's communication, though it is not so much an avenue different from the rest as the instrument through which the other and richer sources of God's revelation are channeled to believers and the agency of the community for distributing what it possesses in common to its individual members. I am thinking of pastoral ministry in the church.

We know that the New Testament does not give us a detailed and literal description of how the earliest disciples of Jesus were organized, but with respect to their organization, this minimal conclusion is beyond controversy. Within the larger circle of followers of Jesus, there was a smaller circle to whom Jesus entrusted a special and distinctive ministry. The earliest community was not homogeneous; within the wider body of disciples there were those chosen for a ministry of leadership, or we might better call it, a pastoral service toward others. Without attempting to specify this office further, let us call it the apostolic ministry, and it is this apostolic ministry which I am proposing as integral to the process of knowing God's revelation. The ministry of leadership developed in different forms in the various cities where Christianity took root, and how it was and should be exercised has long been a subject of controversy, but this controversy will not occupy us here.

It is not that the apostles and their successors have new material of their own to add to the scriptures, the sacraments and the other works of God through the centuries. Their function is rather to hold together what comes from all other sources. They are the voice and agency of the community. Without the apostolic ministry believers are set adrift in the midst of all the diversity of sources we have been describing. This is not to suggest that apostolic ministry is the only or the most important bond which holds believers together (the Holy Spirit, the Eucharist and the Gospel are obviously more important), but only that without the specific contribution apostolic ministry makes, the other loftier bonds cannot keep believers together in one body, confessing the same faith and collaborating in the same common project. The binding of a book is not its most excellent feature, but without it there would be nothing but loose pages.

Whatever may be said in theory, twenty centuries of experience have demonstrated that an authoritative ministry of guidance is needed to preserve unity in faith. Without it each believer is left before a bewildering variety of opinions. In fact, as we noted in another context, the believer's choice will be that of deciding which expert to follow, if he wants intellectual grounds for his position, or of following his own personal and highly subjective inclinations and ignoring any evidence that does not fit. There is a world of difference between the expert and the apostolic minister. The former can only speak for himself, and the grounds for accepting his opinion can only be his personal competence; the latter speaks in the name of the community, through an authorization which comes from the community, delivering a message which is not proper to the minister but transmitted through him from the whole, unified community of Jesus and hence mediately from Jesus himself.

Linkage to Jesus is in and through the community, or to take up the imagery of St. Paul, it is only by being joined to each other in the unity of one body that members are joined to their head. To lose our unity with the body, is to be severed from its head. The expert as such is not an agent of the community, though his task is necessary to it. His primary loyalty as an expert must be to his own very particular vision, otherwise he will compromise the distinctive service only he can render. The unity of the church is not his prime responsibility, on the contrary it is often his task to prevent an oversimplified unity which does not do justice to the complexity of evidence. Consequently, there is need of a service of unity, a ministry directly concerned with keeping the flock of Christ together, and this is the function of the apostolic ministry. Without it, as we observed above, history has taught us that the community fragments.

Over the course of the centuries, especially during periods of turmoil and unusual dissention in matters of faith and practice, the apostolic ministry has been exercised in the form of gatherings of the leadership (bishops) from all over the world (ecumenical councils) to provide the kind of exceptional guidance needed in the circumstances. The product of these councils has been authoritative statements of Christian faith in the form of the great creeds, e.g., the Nicene Creed, and concise formulations of essential Christian belief. To most Christians such statements of dogma have been regarded as authentic and irreversible expressions of the faith and life of the whole community. Unlike the opinions of experts, which stand or fall on the wisdom and skill of their authors, the weight of the entire community stands behind these crystallizations of faith and so they are guaranteed by the Holy Spirit, from whom the life and the faith of the community ultimately derive. The first seven of these ecumenical councils were quite universally accepted by Christians as definitive guidance. Since the eleventh century, however, no universal agency of apostolic ministry has been recognized by all Christians, but Roman Catholics believe that the universal ministry conferred by Christ on St. Peter continues in the papal office.

For all Christians, as indeed for all interested parties, documents and decisions of the apostolic ministry are an indispensable source for understanding Christianity. Many Christians go much further, recognizing in them an authority which goes beyond the competence or even the faith of their authors. They must be included among the sources whereby God makes himself known to his people and as an important part of the catholic view of revelation.

How unfortunate it is that apostolic ministry is often seen as something negative and restrictive! Encouragement and facilitation are at least as much the duty of leaders as prohibition. Like the rest of us, bishops and others who exercise a ministry of leadership often do so badly; they may be fearful of new developments, obstinate in their outdated ways, vain, insensitive, and in a word, subject to all the defects we find in others; but in itself their office is very positive. Its goal is to channel the riches of the Christian heritage to others, to minister, that is, to serve others with what Christ has passed on to them; its only negative duty is to keep us out of blind alleys so that Christian life may continue to flow in the direction given it from the beginning. It is the agency whereby the community preserves its continuity and identity, and hence its vital relationship with its origins, not substituting itself for the other great agencies of Christian life, like the sacred scriptures and the sacraments, but keeping them together. Nor does it follow that the appropriate response to ecclesial leadership on the part of those who accept it as belonging to their faith commitment to Jesus, is lock step obedience. Paul confronted Peter when he saw that he was wrong in his dealings with Gentile converts.[13] Sincere criticism can be a better and more faithful response to church authority than passive and thoughtless submission. Pastors are not called to think and act in place of the faithful but to keep the community together (not in every detail but basically) as a community.

Many are reluctant to grant any authority to the official teaching of apostolic ministry within the church, other than the authority we acknowledge in any expert who has demonstrated competence in a particular field. They feel that submission to any other kind of authority is an abdication of personal responsibility. But a twofold misunderstanding may lurk behind such an attitude. First, for the believer the church community is greater than the sum of its parts. If the official teaching is the voice of the community itself, then its authority is not measured by the personal competence of the minister but by the credibility of the church as the body of Christ, animated by the Holy Spirit. What is called for is not submission to the person of the minister but the submission of all Christians, ordinary believer or minister alike, to the invisible Source of the church's life. Authority does not originate with the minister but passes through him.

But there is often a second less fundamental misunderstanding involved. It consists in an exaggerated notion of the authority claimed for church teaching. Authority does not have to be absolute in order to be genuine and the vast majority of official teaching is not proposed as absolute. It is offered as guidance for the present without laying claim to completeness and finality. It is testimony to the communitarian quality of all Christian life. We do not pursue our search for the Lord and for his kingdom in isolation but in company with our brothers and sisters. The community's guidance is of great value but it is not the end of searching but a signpost along the way. Roman Catholics and many other Christians do affirm that the apostolic ministry can on occasion make decisions which are final and irreformable but such decisions are rare. Moreover even in such rare cases and much more in the ordinary process of teaching, there is no suggestion that all has been said that can be said, or even that what has been said cannot be said better.

It is significant that the most decisive dogmatic statements are frequently expressed negatively, which is to say that they do not state what must be believed, but reject an understanding which is irreconcilable with the faith and experience of the church. Paradoxically, the negative form is less restrictive. It warns us away from a detour, which would detach us from the essential faith of the community but it leaves the path of further reflection open.

In summary, we have been arguing through these pages that there are many sources of God's revelation. We have singled out four without suggesting that the list is exhaustive: the sacred scriptures, the liturgy, the total experience of the church community and the exercise of apostolic ministry. The Christian community is not catholic unless it is open to all of these sources.

If all of these sources are accepted will the confusion we spoke of in the beginning of this section be completely removed? Of course not. A perfectly clear and ordered picture of God's revelation of himself through Christ in the Holy Spirit would be totally disproportionate to the mysterious reality involved. The Christian church is a people on the march, not one settled down in its final destination. Believers must live with very partial answers to the questions their faith provokes. But between perfect clarity and utter confusion there are intermediate points. Clarity and definiteness attained by restricting the focus to only a part of the light God has provided is attained prematurely and at the expense of the fullness of truth. But a confusion which leaves one bewildered and unable to move drains the energy out of Christian living. The church of Christ will be catholic if she keeps all the sources of God's revelation in lively interaction with each other. Within her communion, we will not need a detailed map of the whole plan of God to guide us, but we will be satisfied with enough light to find our way, step by step.

Notes

1. 1 Tm. 2:5,6.

2. "Towards a Fundamental Theological Interpretation of Vatican II," *Theological Studies,* Vol. 40 (Dec. 1979), pp. 716-27.

3. Eph. 1:10.

4. See, for example, James D.G. Dunn, *Unity And Diversity In The New Testament: an Inquiry Into The Character Of Earliest Christianity* (Phila.: Westminster Press, 1977).

5. See Paul J. Achtemeier, Raymond Brown, eds., M*Ary In The New Testament: A Collaborative Assessment By Protestant And Roman Catholic Scholars,* sponsored by U.S. Lutheran—Roman Catholic Dialogue (Phila.: Fortress Press, 1978). Also, Raymond E. Brown, Karl P. Donfried and John Reumann, eds., *Peter In The New Testament: A Collaborative Assessment By Protestant And Roman Catholic Scholars* (Minneapolis: Augsburg Publ. House, 1973).

6. Cf. Jn. Ch.7.

7. A very scholarly study of these different senses of scripture is found in Henri de Lubac, S.J., *Exégèse Médiévale: Les Quatre Sens De L'ecriture,* 4 vols. (Paris: Aubier, 1959).

8. "Justice in the World," 1971 Synod of Bishops. Text in *The Pope Speaks,* Vol. 16 (1971), p. 377.

9. Mt. 25:31-46.

10. Mt. 16:13-20.

11. Jn. 21:25.

12. 1 Cor. 10:11.

13. See Gal. 2:11-14.

Chapter Five

Catholicity in Context

As we come to the end of our journey let's circle back to where we began. There is always danger of forgetting what we are looking for as we become absorbed in searching. What we have been looking for is the demand for catholicity which our times make upon Christians to an unprecedented degree. But perhaps the greatest enemy in responding to this invitation is a naive and oversimplified notion of what catholicity means as applied to the church and the mission of Christ. The cause of catholicity has more to fear from its friends than from its enemies.

It makes me uncomfortable when people agree too readily with the thesis of this book. I am afraid they understand it simplistically as a rather obvious appeal for openmindedness or tolerance in the secular mode, or worse still, as a rootless, unscriptural call to abandon everything within the

Christian tradition which is firm and sharp enough to divide people from each other and therefore meaningful enough to be worth defending. It is precisely a reputation for this kind of theological and moral spinelessness on the part of the main line churches which is largely responsible for their decline in membership and influence, while narrower, more sectarian churches thrive. No one who has read earlier chapters will suspect that this book puts forth such an understanding of catholicity, but I would like to devote this final chapter to what is specific to the catholicity of Christ's church, what distinguishes it from any other form of openness or universality. I want to fit the quality of being catholic into the total picture of the church in all its essential elements. The catholicity we have been advocating is no generalized broadmindedness or cosmopolitan spirit but a quality proper to the church of Christ which believers have been confessing since the early creeds were formulated.

That catholicity is not an abstraction. It is anchored in the concrete reality of Jesus of Nazareth and any flexibility which weakens or obscures this linkage is excluded in principle. Moreover it is not some purely spiritual linkage with Jesus, some common cause with him or sharing in his ideals, but fellowship with him, risen and alive, within a human community, composed of real men and women—a unique community, to be sure, but nonetheless genuinely human.

The way I propose to situate catholicity within the total context of the church is to relate it to those other characteristics which Christians have believed are essential to the church and which are often referred to as "the marks of the church." Since at least the fourth century believers have recognized four qualities as describing the church of Jesus Christ. According to the Niceno-Constantinopolitan creed, the church of Jesus Christ is "one, holy, catholic and apostolic".[1] These qualities pertain to the church by the inner necessity of her own life, because she is the body of the risen Christ, the extension of his own presence and action. Therefore, they can never be totally absent. Still what the church is by nature, she is imperfectly at present. She must become in fact what she already is in principle. She is a pilgrim people. She does not come fully formed from the hand of God but must struggle through the centuries to realize the potential she had from the beginning, much as any living being grows into its own complete identity. But unlike other living beings the growth of the church is more than the unfolding of actual resources embedded in her from the start; ultimately the Holy Spirit of God is the source of the church's vitality and adaptability, introducing an element of surprise and unpredictability into the process. Growth is not mechanical but organic and an organism responds to the needs of its environment. One function may develop in spurts while others are dormant. So with the church of Jesus Christ. There is no reason to assume that the four essential qualities will develop in parallel fashion or at the same pace, but since they are different potentialities of the same divine life they are inseparable. To sacrifice one for the sake of promoting another would denature even the one supposedly favored. Let us explore the relationship between catholicity and the other marks or essential characteristics of the church of Christ.

Catholicity and Unity in Tension

First, then, unity. Unity and catholicity stand in dialectical tension with each other. They are like two opposite poles to which a rope is fastened or better two teams in a tug of war, because the rope in my analogy is not stationary but represents the vibrant and mobile career of the church. If too much pressure is applied to one pole, the other is in danger of being uprooted; if too little, the rope will become slack and lifeless. The secret of healthy tone is adequate pressure exerted from both sides. Catholicity is a centrifugal force sweeping out from the center to reach a wider field. It is the church's power of expansion, her restlessness within the boundaries of the present, her dissatisfaction with what has already been achieved and her fascination for what is outside. Unity is a centripetal force drawing in what is scattered and diverse, integrating the parts into a whole, fitting them together so that they can work with each other and one life can energize them all. Its mission is to consolidate, to separate the gold from the dross in what catholicity brings in, to preserve what is valuable in the past, to prevent expansion from turning into disintegration.

Without unity there can be no catholicity. If the church should lose its own identity and integrity there would be nothing to spread and no place to bring new acquisitions. When centrifugal force is not balanced by its centripetal counterpart everything is scattered. Earlier we compared the church to an expanding circle surrounding an historical point; the circle is continually widening (its catholicity) but if the compass were not anchored in that historical point there would be no circle but only chaotic lines. To be completely open is to be empty.

On the other hand, the converse is not true. Unity is not dependent upon catholicity. A closed society can be thoroughly unified; indeed the less open and dynamic a society is, the more easily it stays together, but the unity which is a mark of Christ's church is not any kind of unity but only one measured to the dimensions of Jesus' mission to all mankind. Keeping people together is not all that difficult if it can be done in terms of their own interests and in opposition to what appears strange and foreign. The catholicity of the church may consequently be a more striking manifestation of the Holy Spirit's presence within her than her extraordinary permanence and survival, but the combination of the two is more remarkable still. The church of Jesus Christ has not preserved her identity by building walls against the outside world and enforcing strict discipline within but while reaching out and adapting herself repeatedly to new situations. Still it is important to remember that adaptation is contingent upon the preservation of unity.

Before going forward let me describe more concretely how unity and catholicity interact. When the church of Christ is faced with new, uncharted territory, whether the newness be as obvious and external as the new continents discovered in the fifteenth century or as subtle and challenging as intellectual progress and cultural change, she has within her make-up two opposite tendencies, both belonging to her nature. The one is eager to embrace the stranger; it wants to incorporate the new territory without delay. This viewpoint is solidly founded in the Christian belief that creation and redemption are both part of the same Divine plan as we explained in the previous chapter. Whatever is good and true anywhere belongs by right within the kingdom of God; neither it nor the kingdom can achieve their full potential apart from one another. The wisdom of ancient Greece, the legal systems and institutions of the Roman empire, the customs of Germanic tribes, the explosion of art and scholarship in the renaissance, the scientific advances of more recent centuries, modern developments in psychology, philosophy and the social sciences—all have appealed irresistibly to the church's centrifugal force, as we have indicated in previous pages. Necessarily so. If Christ died "to gather into one all the dispersed children of God"[2] and "to bring all things in the heavens and on earth into one under (his) headship",[3] then all of these belong to Christ, and the church, which is his agent, must claim them for him.

On the other hand entrance into the kingdom is always by way of conversion. Nothing becomes part of the kingdom of God by the mere fact of its creation but only by a new and second birth. There is need for turning (which is what conversion means), a change of direction. This implies that the natural dynamism of the creature cannot carry it into the kingdom of God. The road is not so straight and easy. If what has just been said applies first and most obviously to human beings, it also applies by extension to the institutions and cultures through which human beings reach out into the world around them and by means of which they form that world according to their own image and communicate their personal vision and values to others. If people need conversion so does their society and all its institutions. The centrifugal tendency responds to the presence of God everywhere since the beginning of time, but the Bible reminds us that God has not been the only actor at work on the historical scene. According to the dramatic account of Genesis, sin and evil gained a foothold in this world of ours from the start, and their dominion has been expanding ever since, never in complete control and never uncontested but always at work. God's response to the power of evil was to provide a radically new beginning in his only Son, Jesus Christ, our Lord. The salvation and sanctification of the world is not a simple continuation of the Divine work of creation, it comes only through the cross of Jesus and it entails a rupture with what has gone before. The second of these opposing tendencies of Christians in the face of new worlds beyond the boundaries of the church responds to this other darker side of the human story, likewise solidly attested by Christian faith. It recognizes that cultures, institutions and achievements of the human spirit are not pure products of people's natural hunger for God. They are also the expression of pride, selfishness, cruelty, and general sinfulness and in any case even at their best are powerless to lead us to the true goal of human existence unless they are joined to Jesus Christ and permeated by his Spirit.

Concretely, then, the unifying or centripetal tendency will be concerned to safeguard tradition. It is the connecting link with Christ. It will be suspicious of what is too congenial to the spirit of the times, too appealing to our nonbelieving contemporaries. As G.K. Chesterton once remarked, in connection with the demand for a church which moves with the times, it takes no effort and no special excellence to do so. What he wanted, Chesterton said, was a church that did not move with the times but moved the times, that was right when the times were wrong. The unifying or centripetal tendency wishes to satisfy this criterion of Chesterton for a church which speaks for God rather than public opinion. It will rein in uncritical enthusiasm which can mistake a passing fad for a new movement in history or accept each new school of thought as the final word on the subject.

The contrast we have sketched above is over simplified, to be sure, but it casts light on a tension that does and should exist within the church between a drive for catholicity and a somewhat opposed concern for unity. What is important is that neither tendency should overpower the other. Christians normally coalesce around one pole or the other with the result that the opposition is not so much theoretical as it is a conflict between different groups with different priorities. What determines our allegiance to one group or the other is probably as much a matter of temperament or the nature of our own responsibilities within the community as of theological argument. But applying the principle we developed at length in Chapter Three, this kind of tension is a positive benefit to the church. The worst thing which could happen is that either side should excommunicate the other. If forces for unity are weak, forces for change and adaptation will become sloppy. It has been suggested, for instance, that the reforms set in motion by the Second Vatican Council would have been more effective if a stronger, more intelligent opposition on the part of conservatives had stood in their way. Instead once the initial intransigence was overcome, victory became too easy and too consistent for progressives; they were able to enact their plans without the corrections which vigorous debate and necessary compromise would have required. On the other hand, when defenders of orthodoxy and the *status quo* are securely in control the result will be stagnation.

I suspect that it is always a minority of Christians who will feel strongly the centrifugal or catholic drive we talked about. Inertia is a powerful factor in religion as elsewhere. Reaching out to what is new calls for a degree of imagination and energy that is usually in short supply; it is much easier to settle for what we already have. No doubt many will be ready to jettison burdensome elements in tradition in favor of easier contemporary practice but that is a far cry from genuine catholicity. The latter is not an escape from the sacrifices of the past but a response to the challenges of the future—seen in the light of faith, faith in a crucified Lord. There will be no easy way to meet them.

But neither is this to suggest that those whose task is to preserve the linkage with the past and thus to safeguard the unity of the church have chosen the path of least resistance. Chrysostom, Athanasius, Thomas More and so many other Christian heroes of the past who suffered exile, persecution and even death in defense of orthodox Christian faith against the prevailing currents of their society are refutation enough of such a notion. In actuality, standing firm in defense of unity and tradition may be more difficult than contesting against them since it lacks the aura of romanticism and heroism which surrounds rebellion.

Paradoxically, it is the defenders of unity and tradition who extend change and innovation into the main body of Christians. Prophets and pioneers tend to be lonely figures. The initiatives they introduce into the community can take flight leaving the ordinary Christians behind, fascinated perhaps but unchanged. How deeply their influence penetrates into the community depends on how unified that community is and how much the vision of the prophet is translated into structures, institutions and practices which guide its rank and file. It was only because it became institutionalized in the Franciscan order that the spirituality of Francis of Assissi transformed the Christian world. Leaders of the community, who must by the nature of their responsibilities be more attentive to the feelings and even to the lassitude or resistances of the majority, perform a task which is indispensable for progress in catholicity. Often they will be exasperatingly slow but it is through their agency that the community at large moves in a new direction. Let me illustrate from recent American church history.

It has been remarked that the Roman Catholic church was able to move more effectively toward eliminating racial barriers and promoting integration precisely because of its hierarchical structure than other churches where centralized authority was lacking. Decisions once made could be implemented. A few charismatic individuals like Martin Luther King and John LaFarge were essential in bringing the moral and religious issue to clarity, but once that vision was seen clearly by the leadership, they were able to bring along the mass of the people and to institutionalize the new vision.

Something similar seems to be happening at present as the American bishops challenge national military strategy in the name of Christian morality. Others have spoken and acted more dramatically; many of these are disappointed that the bishops have not gone further in condemning nuclear weaponry, but it seems clear that the entrance of the bishops so forcefully into the national debate on the issue[4] has reached deeper into the community than individual initiatives ever could, especially since the latter could be dismissed as extreme and eccentric. No one imagines that the majority of American Catholics will change their thinking and practice quickly or completely in keeping with the bishops' lead but a new direction has been given to Catholic thinking on moral issues and its effects will spread quietly and imperceptibly in years to come, especially since the organic and authoritative structure of the Catholic community enables official teaching to permeate its institutions.

Let me propose a test case for the relationship between unity and catholicity from fairly recent history. The nineteenth century was dominated at least in Europe by a struggle between liberalism and conservatism. Granted that the terms are ambiguous and the historical situation was endlessly complex, a rough and admittedly oversimplified sketch of that struggle will illustrate the point.

It would be difficult to exaggerate the importance of the French revolution for Europe and for the rest of the world under its political and cultural influence. The principles which came to expression in France during the catastrophic events at the close of the eighteenth century were the most radical challenge to the foundations of European society in many centuries. Under the motto of "Liberté, égalité, fraternité," a surge of energy swept across Europe which was to overturn not only monarchies but also economic, social, cultural and religious institutions which had been taken for granted since the middle ages. The name of that energy was freedom: a passionate concern for the rights of individual persons in the face of the social institutions, whether of church or state. Politically, governments seesawed back and forth between the older authoritarian forms and republics in the new mode but the underlying force of the movement was irresistible and gradually it won out everywhere.

Within the church the nineteenth century was a time of bitter conflict between the defenders of the old order and those believers who saw great value in the new trends, value thoroughly consistent with Christian faith. Perhaps Félicité de Lammenais typifies the latter, the "liberal" Catholics with their eyes on the future and on the positive side of the new civilization and Pius IX in his later years exemplifies the opposite, conservative bias. No doubt few individuals could be classified as belonging wholly to either camp, but seen as tendencies rather than as clearly elaborated positions, the division surely existed and it corresponds, I believe, to the dialectical tension between unity and catholicity within the church of Christ.

It would be hard today not to regret the dominance of the conservatives in the church of the nineteenth century. Many of the condemnations voiced in Pius IX's "Syllabus of Errors," a collection of propositions attributed to modern (i.e. mid-nineteenth century) times and censured by the Pope, are a painful embarrassment to Catholics today. The excessively cautious and negative approach to scientific and philosophical movements of more recent times on the part of official Catholicism; the isolation of theology from other branches of human life and thought; the association of Christianity with the past rather than the future; the tendency to side with authoritarian and reactionary governments in order to defend religious privileges: all of these products of conservative dominance have inflicted wounds on the Christian community from which we still suffer. It seems clear that the pendulum swung too far in the direction of unity during the nineteenth century at the expense of catholicity.

Yet as we approach the end of the twentieth century, it is clear that the liberal vision, which seemed so appealing a century and a half ago was deeply flawed. Before it won the field it could be viewed in a rosy glow but once it triumphed, cracks in the surface began to appear. Liberal republics were supposed to assure the rights of individuals but in fact they provided opportunity for the strong to benefit at the expense of the weak. The authority of older religious and social institutions was weakened but to a large extent economic power filled the vacuum. Monopolistic capitalism has widened rather than narrowed the gap between the rich and the poor, those capable of exercising their individual rights and those impeded not by law and tradition but by lack of resources. Freedom of speech and of the press was to remove the barriers to mature, independent human development and better education. To some extent it has done so but what was not foreseen was the watering down of culture and education that has occurred in the western world, the controlling influence of the lowest common denominator in a society where the factor which determines what is taught, published or communicated is its appeal to the largest number of paying customers.

The point is not to denigrate the liberal ideals symbolized by the French revolution. They constitute a significant achievement for humanity and one from which there can be no retreat. It is to recognize that the struggle between liberals and conservatives during the nineteenth century was not a conflict between light and darkness. Both factions were defending one-sidedly a part of the truth, and it was not desirable that either faction should win easily or completely.

Our interest here is not in the whole history of the conflict between a new "liberal" society coming to birth in the nineteenth century and the older civilization it was replacing, but only in that conflict in so far as it was carried on within the church. The catholic impulse was to embrace the new demand for liberty as a blood relative rather than a stranger. It was

willing to sever the ties with tottering monarchies and outdated social institutions and to entrust the church's welfare to ordinary people rather than
to the old aristocracy. Those ties had provided support; without them the
future was threatening and uncertain, but the support had become a lia-
bility. If the church was to move effectively into the new civilization, she
would have to accept the pain and sacrifice of jettisoning much of the past
and integrating the new democratic spirit into her life and institutions.

Nor was this a grudging acceptance for the sake of expediency. The
liberal reformers found elements in the bedrock of Christian tradition
which were more friendly to the new society than the old. For instance,
the doctrine that faith is a free gift of God, which cannot be imposed from
without is more congenial to the democratic political institutions of the
nineteenth century than to the authoritarian societies of earlier times. The
separation of religious and secular authority freed Christians, lay and cleri-
cal, for a purer and more authentic spirituality and apostolate than was possible in the ambiguous relationship between church and state in feudal
times. Furthermore, it can be argued that separation between church and
state—a principle dear to the liberal reformers—harks back to a Christian
innovation which contrasted with the mixture of religious and secular authority in the Roman empire, among the Germanic tribes and even in Israel. Power within the church derives from Jesus Christ, not from any political institutions. The situation of Christians in a secular, liberal society
resembled the condition of Christians in apostolic times better than the
dubiously privileged status after Constantine and consequently brought
with it an invitation to a more evangelical Christianity. The "Declaration
of the Rights of Man" (1789), which symbolized the ideals if not the actuality of the French revolution, owed more to Christian belief in the worth
of each individual human being, created by God and redeemed by the
blood of Christ, than it did to the Enlightenment, and it deserved to be
embraced by the church in its essential outline and intention.

All of this has been assimilated into Catholic thought and practice in the
twentieth century, imperfectly, to be sure, but to a degree which would
have shocked nineteenth century conservatives beyond imagination. The
"Declaration on Religious Freedom" of the Second Vatican Council, sub-

titled "On the Right of the Person and of Communities to Social and Civil Freedom in Matters Religious," is the most official and authoritative acceptance on the part of the Roman Catholic church of the goals for which liberal Catholics struggled for more than a century. But also the perspective which governs the other documents of the Council, especially those on the church, ecumenism and the relationship of the church to the modern world; the radical change of style and substance in the new code of church law; such recent institutions as parochial and diocesan councils, which have turned the church away from the rigidity of the post-Reformation past toward a freer, more open mentality: all of these things make it plain that catholicity has triumphed. The church has baptized the liberal revolution. Or more exactly, under the stimulus of the liberal revolution the church of Christ has been forced to reexamine her own heritage and has uncovered treasures there which would have gone unnoticed and undeveloped had not the historical circumstances of the recent past called attention to them. A living being grows not just by taking in what a new environment offers, but because the new enviroment provokes an internal reaction and latent resources expand in interaction with the changed environment. Over the portal of many a European church today is engraved the motto of the revolution, "Liberté, égalité, fraternité," a dramatic symbol that the church of the twentieth century has in large measure embraced the liberal revolution of the nineteenth century, thereby proving her catholicity, but she has done so after the fashion of a living organism, growing from within in contact with what is outside, expanding her own distinctive tradition and integrating new and old into one continuous story, thereby preserving her unity. Couldn't the process have been easier and less painful?

Couldn't the Christian values embedded in the new civilization coming to birth in the nineteenth century have been recognized sooner and accepted with better grace? Perhaps, if Christians and their adversaries had been wiser and holier, but what was at stake was not a conflict of ideas but a conflict between historical groups and history never comes in pure form. It is relatively easy at this point in time to sift out the theoretical issues; in actuality the liberal principles accepted by the Second Vatican Council made their debut in history as part of an historical matrix which was aggressively pagan, hostile to Christianity and often consciously intent on uprooting every vestige of the Christian heritage. For the Christian church to have accepted the movement as it existed concretely would have been a gross and unthinkable betrayal of faith.

We can sympathize with the impatience of liberal Catholics at the slowness of church leaders to recognize the elements of truth and value lodged in the revolutionary society coming to birth. Still it is arguable that the church leadership was more in contact with the social realities of the time than far sighted intellectuals, whose vision would be justified in the future but in their contemporary situation were ahead of the times. Academics and prophets are best at perceiving the underlying issues at stake; community leaders may be closer to the real situation of ordinary people, which involves much more than intellectual issues. It takes a long time for such a large group as the Christian church to move in a new direction without disintegrating or losing values built up in the past. Only because the community was held together by its pastors was it able to move as a whole in the new direction. The influence of those who withdrew in frustration and went their separate way was dissipated. None of this excuses the blindness and obstinacy of many in positions of authority but a large measure of patience and tolerance is the price of unity. When the unity is ultimately with Christ and two millenia of his followers, it is a price worth paying.

What we have said just above is largely a matter of tactics. Theoretically, too, the liberal revolution of the nineteenth century called for critical evaluation rather than simple acceptance, as we have pointed out earlier in this chapter. From a doctrinal standpoint its most serious defect was the shallow understanding of human existence it promoted. The typical liberal was guided by a naive optimism, a romantic confidence in the goodness of human nature and the power of humanity to solve all its problems, if only we were rid of superstition and the deadening weight of tradition. This clashes with Christian belief in the universal sinfulness of mankind and subsequent history has been kinder to Christian realism than to the romanticism of nineteenth century liberals. More fundamentally, the liberal movement tended to be a humanism with little or no place for God and less for the basic doctrines of Christian faith. True, many of its advocates defended a form of religious sentiment but the Christianity they championed rested on a very selective reading of the New Testament. Is it any wonder that Christians did not welcome with open arms such a vision of life?

The purpose of this incursion into history, let me remind the reader, has been to illustrate the dialectical relationship between catholicity and unity. In the nineteenth century the church of pre-revolutionary times met the rising tide of a new civilization; because the church is catholic, she had to open up to what was new; but the condition for doing so without losing identity was her unity. Neither the most enthusiastic advocates of the new liberal trends nor the reactionary defenders of the old regime offered sound advice. Only the slow and painful process which involved both the centrifugal force of catholicity and the centripetal force of unity offered real hope for the future.

Since the church can only be catholic to the extent she is one, the greater the demand for catholicity the stronger her unity must be. If what we have argued in this book is true, namely that our times call for catholicity more urgently than ever before then it follows that unity is more essential than ever. In a period of stability when choices are limited there is less strain on unity; in a period of intense activity and change, unity is both harder to maintain and more necessary. Notice it is unity not uniformity at issue here. A centralized, monolythic unity may be easier to preserve, but if we have established anything in the course of this study, it is that such a unity is not suited to the rich diversity of the church of Christ. On the other hand the greater the diversity the more delicate yet the more necessary is the task of maintaining unity.

The renowned American sociologist of religion, Robert Bellah, recently made an observation which goes to the heart of what I am saying here.[5] He was discussing the division of religions into three types as proposed by Ernst Troeltsch, which has become classic in religious sociology: the sect, which in our terms would be the opposite of catholicity, since it is narrow and restrictive by definition; mysticism, which is the opposite of unity, since it is amorphous and indefinite; and finally the "church" model, which brings together both unity and catholicity, since it involves tangible institutional agencies unlike the mystical model without the rigidity of the sect.

Troelsch did not regard these as three equal options; he saw that only the "church" model has the breadth and solidity necessary for long term and large scale survival. Bellah goes on to warn his hearers that the effectiveness of Christian religion depends upon its survival as a church.

Significantly, Bellah's warning was addressed to a gathering of Roman Catholic theologians. If any church has been concerned with the institutional structures needed to make believers a "church" in Troelsch' sense, it is the church of Rome, but in the anti-institutional climate of recent decades, Bellah felt that Roman Catholics were in danger of forgetting this truth so central to their own tradition.

Bellah's experience resonates with my own. When I began writing this book my intention was to preserve a widely ecumenical perspective and to avoid anything that would limit the usefulness of these pages to Roman Catholics, but as the work has progressed I have become more and more convinced of the crucial importance of that specific and distinctive contribution the Roman Catholic tradition makes to the wider catholicity of Christ's church. Without visible structures of unity, Christian believers cannot become a community of faith and love, open to a world expanding in every cultural dimension but drawn more tightly together by communication and interdependence. Visible agencies of unity are not the loftiest or the most attractive elements of Christ's church, they are, nonetheless indispensable.

Unity of a Special Kind: Apostolicity

We can be brief about the two remaining marks of the church. Apostolicity specifies the unity peculiar to the church of Jesus Christ. There are different kinds of unity; only one of them satisfies the demand for unity within the church: that of an historical movement. It is not the unity of an idea or a school of thought; it is more than sharing in the same mystical experience or in the same spirit, even if that spirit is the Holy Spirit of God. The unity of the church is not simply unity with God; more immediately it is unity with the man, Jesus of Nazareth, in all his historical particularity. The church must connect subsequent generations of believers not just with the divinity of Jesus but also with his humanity, or better with his divinity through his humanity. At no point in history is it possible to bypass the human in order to go directly to God. As it was only in the human words and gestures of Jesus, spoken in a particular language, and colored by the customs of a particular race, that God was revealed to the earliest disciples, so later generations make contact with Jesus through the preaching and writing, the living and acting of their predecessors in the faith, all of it marked with the limitations and particularity of those believers. The name of this connecting link stretching back through the centuries to Jesus of Nazareth is apostolic succession, and Christians have long considered it essential to the kind of unity necessary in the church.

There is no intrinsic necessity that these particular twelve, whom Jesus gathered around himself, should be the foundation stones of the Christian church, any more than it was intrinsically necessary for God to become man in Israel in the first century, but given the kind of intervention God chose to make in the affairs of the human family and the kind of religion Christianity is, linkage with these particular men is essential to authentic Christianity.

If Christians could be satisfied with any kind of unity, one could imagine a unification of all who describe themselves as Christians in a new consensus independent of everything in the past. Conceivably some new, secular project, such as the establishment of world government, international disarmament and the elimination of war, might be sufficiently appealing to win the allegiance of all and overcome the divisions of the past, but this would not be the unity of the church of Jesus Christ, which we profess as Christians. The latter is a unity of continuity, not exclusively of the present nor looking only to the future but also rooted in the past. The only unity worth having among Christians is one that unites us with Jesus Christ, and with Jesus not simply as we know him at present by faith, glorious and risen from the dead, but also as he made himself known in the historical reality of his life on earth, in the language of our own very earthly condition, the memory of which has been passed on to us in the same way as other human memories through the community which came to know him and shared their experience with following generations. To put it graphically the unity at issue is not merely horizontal but vertical. It aims to gather together not just all who are living now but to join those who are living now with those who have gone before and those who will come after. It is a unity in time as well as in space, the unity of a story whose climax is the life, death and resurrection of Jesus, prepared for earlier and carried on afterwards in that subsequent generations are being invited to take part in the one continuing action.

Let us pull together the strands of our argument in this chapter. We have been connecting catholicity with the other essential characteristics of Christ's church. Catholicity depends on unity; the church can only be catholic insofar as she is one. Apostolicity describes the kind of unity essential to the church, so it is only insofar as believers today share in the same faith and are joined in the same fellowship and play their part in the same continuing story as the apostles and their successors that the church can be catholic. A kind of catholicity or worldwide diffusion of people calling themselves Christians might exist without such communion with believers of the past but it would not be the catholicity we have been talking about in this book, because what was spread throughout the world, however admirable, would not be the church of Jesus Christ.

This needs to be said more plainly than ever in our day of unprecedented demand for openness on the part of Christians. Just as it was the fact of diversity in faith with the rise of Gnosticism that originally forced Christians to add the adjective "apostolic" to the description of the church of Jesus Christ in the creeds, so the religious and cultural mobility of our own times calls for renewed emphasis on apostolicity as essential to the church. The other side of the coin to the thesis of this book about the urgent need for catholicity is the need to remain firmly rooted in the apostolic tradition. Apostolicity is the life line of the church; to let go of that connecting link for the sake of reaching further into the new civilization would be to give up the whole project.

Catholicity and Holiness

Which brings us to the last essential quality of Christ's church: holiness. Holiness is last in our treatment of the marks of the church but first and most important in other respects. The earliest description of the church in the creeds is that she is "holy," and even before the creeds, the New Testament accentuates the holiness of the church not only explicitly as in the letter to the Ephesians where holiness is seen as the purpose for which Christ died,[6] but implicitly as the meaning of the whole drama of redemption. For fundamentally holiness is nothing but unity with God. Ultimately there is no reason for the church to exist other than to draw humanity into unity with the Father, through the Son in the Spirit.

When we speak of holiness we think instinctively of good conduct. A holy person is one whose life manifests high moral standards. The emphasis is on doing rather than on being, but we need to be reminded that holy living flows from a more fundamental kind of holiness in the understanding of Christians and indeed of religious people of almost all traditions. God is real; his contact with us is not just that of a teacher or a moral guide but of a living person as real as the air we breathe though infinitely more mysterious. To be one with him is not just to be influenced by his teaching but to be joined with him in fact. Religion as opposed to ethics, which too often functions as its substitute, aims at contact with God that is ontological as well as psychological. It is person-to-person relationship, sharing of life, communion with God. Christianity ambitions more than changing our patterns of living; it is satisfied with nothing less than insertion into the life eternally interchanged between the three divine persons. Holy living is the overflow into action of more radical oneness with God, as such it belongs to the holiness of the church. However, so many obstacles can intervene between the radical holiness effected by Baptism and its expression in Christ-like conduct that it seems wiser to concentrate on the real as opposed to the moral unity of believers with God in reflecting on the holiness of the church. The Holy Spirit will only influence our conduct to the extent that we freely cooperate, and so many factors, conscious and unconscious, social and individual, such as ignorance and prejudice, ideology and ingrained habits transmitted over the centuries can blunt and deflect the Spirit's action. If the channels of communication with God in Christ are kept open, fruits of sanctity will flourish according to the mysterious plan of God. Church people will never be able to predict how and where this action of the Holy Spirit will manifest itself and when it does their understanding of it will be imperfect. The ecclesial task is only to preserve the linkage, to keep the channels from silting up. The rest is up to God.

If unity is the most visible mark of the church, holiness is the most invisible, since holiness is closest to the invisible Source of all vitality within the church. It is most immediately in contact with the ineffable mystery which has come among us in the person of Jesus of Nazareth. True, it must bear fruit in very earthly and concrete actions, and the soundness of the fruit produced is the test Jesus has given us for discerning where the Holy Spirit is present.[7] Nonetheless we are always in danger of confusing our standards of what ought to be with God's and subjecting God's plans to our expectations. Since holiness is most immediately a question of what God himself is doing in our world, it is the most elusive of all the church's attributes. It may be fairly easy to know what makes for unity among believers or expands the church's influence beyond her present borders but when it comes to discerning the action of the Holy Spirit the greatest humility is called for and the last word will belong to mystery.

Holiness is consequently the least apt of the church's characteristics to mark out the path believers ought to follow although Christians have been tempted since the early centuries to bypass other agencies and look directly to holiness as the infallible sign of God's will and presence. The first century Donatists, for example, separated themselves from the main body of Christians because the Donatists elevated the holiness of the minister into a necessary condition for the validity of the ministry. And how many other Savonerolas over the centuries since have diverted Christians into at least bizarre and often destructive detours by force of the holiness—real or imagined—of their own lives. Today especially, the temptation is widespread. An appeal to the felt presence of God can overrule any objection. But this is unwise for the reason pointed out above. The very thing which makes holiness the loftiest and most important quality of the church makes it the most intangible and the most open to deception, namely its direct connection with God. How can we identify the Holy Spirit's action in the complex reality of experience and separate it out from purely human factors? The closer anything is to God the more obscure.

> The wind blows where it will.
> You hear the sound it makes
> but you do not know where it comes from or where it goes.
> So it is with everyone begotten of the Spirit.[8]

We do not know concretely what God is doing in our world or even what he wants to do. The instruments he uses to do his work will almost certainly fail to meet our specifications. In the last instance all we can do is preserve our linkage to God in Christ; the direction and final outcome is in his hands.

The Christian life begins and ends in faith. If we knew exactly what God was aiming at we could organize our part in the project with greater assurance, but both in its source and in its goal the whole Christian enterprise, individual and social, depends on an act of faith. We can be reasonably clear about the means but the end escapes our understanding and our control. All the agencies of the Christian community exist only to serve as a channel whereby the action of God—always unpredictable and often upsetting to our norms of judgement—reaches people. This is not to confine the holiness of the church to some private and invisible zone, because the God who acts through her is the God who has become incarnate and is at work in all the very earthly, visible and social dimensions of human life but it is to relativize our understanding of what is happening and our judgement of its success. The church is engaged in a project which she did not originate and which she does not fully understand. She is collaborating with an unseen partner and the goal, holiness, is correspondingly hard to measure. When all is said and done catholicity means extending an influence which is not our own and opening the way to results we cannot anticipate; it is a work of faith.

Holiness is the innermost property of the church of Christ, the main spring of the whole ecclesial project, the soul which gives life to everything else, since it is the action of the Spirit of God. Without it no amount of unity, no fidelity to apostolic tradition and no outreach to the wider world would be of any real worth. On the other hand, without unity, apostolicity and catholicity, the saving power of the Holy Spirit would be disengaged from the world of men and women, disembodied. If we image the four traditionally accepted marks of the church as rings of light radiating out from a candle, holiness is closest to the flame and catholicity is farthest away gradually mingling with the darkness, but the rings are not stationary. They intermingle and fluctuate and, in fact, they are nothing more than the light of the same candle seen from different directions. We can separate them mentally and it helps to do so because the mission of the church is many faceted with different aspects requiring attention at different times and in different situations, but it is important to recall that they are inseparable. If the thesis of this book is correct, catholicity is the special imperative of our times and our times are uncovering dimensions of catholicity unsuspected by believers in the past but catholicity only makes sense in the total setting of the church of Christ as the creeds have described her: one, holy, catholic and apostolic.

Notes

1. Clarkson et al., *The Church Teaches: Documents Of The Church In English Translation* (St. Louis: B. Herder, 1955) p.2.

2. Jn. 11:52.

3. Eph. 1:10.

4. Cf. *The Challenge Of Peace: God's Promise And Our Response; A Pastoral Letter On War And Peace*, National Conference of Catholic Bishops, May 3, 1983.

5. "Religion and Power in America Today," *Proceedings Of The 37th Annual Convention Of The Catholic Theological Society Of America*, 1982.

6. Eph. 5:25.

7. cf. Mt. 7:16-20.

8. Jn. 3:8.